SAVING K-12

What Happened to Our Public Schools?

How Do We Fix Them?

BRUCE DEITRICK PRICE

ANAPHORA LITERARY PRESS
BROWNSVILLE, TEXAS

ANAPHORA LITERARY PRESS
1898 Athens Street
Brownsville, TX 78520
https://anaphoraliterary.com

Book design by Anna Faktorovich, Ph.D.

Printed in the United States of America, United Kingdom and in Australia on acid-free paper.

Cover Photo by Philippe Put: www.ineedair.org.

For information about Bruce Deitrick Price, see pages 182-185.

Published in 2017 by Anaphora Literary Press

SAVING K-12:
What Happened to Our Public Schools? How Do We Fix Them?
Bruce Deitrick Price—1st edition.

Library of Congress Control Number: 2017946111

Library Cataloging Information
Price, Bruce Deitrick, 1941-, author.
    Saving K-12 / Bruce Deitrick Price
    188 p. ; 9 in.
    ISBN 978-1-68114-361-3 (softcover : alk. paper)
    ISBN 978-1-68114-362-0 (hardcover : alk. paper)
    ISBN 978-1-68114-363-7 (e-book)
1. Education—Secondary.
2. Education—Teaching Methods & Materials—General.
3. Education—Educational Policy & Reform.
LB5-3640: Theory and practice of education
373: Secondary education

SAVING K-12

What Happened to Our Public Schools?

How Do We Fix Them?

_____

BRUCE DEITRICK PRICE

CONTENTS

INTRODUCTION

The two most challenging questions in education are: why do our public schools settle for so much mediocrity and inefficiency; and how can we fix the situation? This book answers both questions.

Please note, my harsh judgment of the public schools is not something I dreamed up. You hear about it in the media every day. The US has 50 million functional illiterates (an unforgivable failure by self-proclaimed experts). Our students don't compete well on international tests. A brainy guy like Bill Gates studied the public schools and said, you know what, the schools are so bad they are a threat to the country's future! In fact, Gates merely repeated what a huge governmental commission concluded in 1983 (the famous *Nation at Risk* report).

If you look back, you find that many smart, sensible people have been writing laments and alarms about public schools for a long time. The decade 1948-1958 witnessed the publication of at least 10 major books with titles such as *Retreat from Learning, Quackery in the Public Schools, Educational Wastelands,* and *Why Johnny Can't Read.*

So we can take it as stipulated, I think, that the nation's public schools ran wildly off the tracks, starting a long time ago.

RUDOLF FLESCH'S BIG MISTAKE

Explaining why this happened, and illuminating the many specific ramifications in the schools, is for me a fascinating quest. Causes and cures are rarely obvious. The Education Establishment (the top people responsible for making the schools mediocre) seem to do everything possible to hide the truth and confuse the debate.

Why Johnny Can't Read was published in 1955, sold eight million copies, and is one of the most important books in American intellectual life. Flesch intended to end the argument about how reading (the essential skill) should be taught. He explained that English, a phonetic language, must be taught phonetically. If you teach it as Sight-Words, you are turning English into Chinese. Flesch thought this idea was so silly, he needed to debunk it only once. We are still paying for this miscalculation.

Virtually every aspect of our K-12 schools is confusing and, I would say, deliberately murky. For that reason, many issues need to be examined again and again. I've thought a good deal about Flesch the last few years. I believe that if he had added a few more paragraphs to his 200-page book, he would have saved millions of Americans from the agony of functional illiteracy.

This book tries to explain everything several times coming from different directions, in different contexts. The goal is that ordinary citizens, with little background in education, will understand all the subtleties.

SAVING THE COUNTRY BY SAVING K-12

If you think of the elite educators at Harvard and Teachers College as brave and noble people, you'll find this book a bit of a shock. It's difficult to conclude that they are noble and brave and have good intentions when you look at the pervasive decay and deliberate dumbing-down in the schools.

I have no grand theories. One simple principle guides everything I say about public schools. Let's educate all children as far as each child can be educated. Why isn't that perfectly reasonable? Surely, anything less is deliberate dumbing-down and a form of child abuse.

The articles are divided into ten sections but it's the sort of collection you can dip into wherever you please and read in any order.

These articles, for the most part, first appeared on many different websites and were focused on a variety of audiences and problems. So you will find that some are grimly serious, some are sarcastic and funny, some are primarily historical, and some are rather scholarly. All of them, I hope, are lively and engaging. All are definitely obsessed with exposing folly and improving education in the public schools.

My fear is that if we don't save our public schools, we won't save much else.

Bruce Deitrick Price
Virginia Beach, VA

1. CULTURE WARS

**Someone does not like our culture.
The evidence is everywhere.**

American Children Are Strangers in a Strange Land

The Education Establishment has managed to separate the country's children from the country. A secret quarantine is in effect; children have been consigned to live in detached bubbles. To a degree rarely seen in history, children are exiles in their own country.

Physically, kids look the same. They are babies in cribs; play in the backyard; have pimples, and become restless teenagers. Little by little, they become adults. You could alter the hairstyle, do a little photo retouching, and all the children would look like the children at the time of the Revolution. Nothing has changed. In appearances, that is.

Inwardly, everything is changed. American children wander forlornly in an alien landscape they know little about and understand less. They have no history, no geography, no math, no science. They've been taught to dislike their country. Instead of knowledge, they've learned detachment and sarcasm, indifference and boredom. They've been systematically deprived of the skills and perspectives that would allow them to enjoy culture or navigate intellectual pursuits.

They are inside the society but curiously outside. Separated from it in the way that a neighborhood's birds and rabbits exist separately from the humans in the neighborhood. They see each other and warily pass; maybe some minor interaction takes place. But birds and rabbits grasp little about what humans are doing or why. Similarly, children stare uncomprehendingly at those strange creatures, adults, living in some parallel life.

The goal for the country's children seems to be the attainment of a pleasant emptiness. White marks on a white wall. It's long been common to say that children's minds are a blank slate, a tabula rasa. But what American public education has achieved is unprecedented: the tabula remains rasa.

How do we describe this state? An intellectual lobotomy? Cognitive neutering? Certainly not all children are stunted in this way. Perhaps 10% or 15% a receive a good education. I'm talking about great majority of average kids. Soon they'll be raising kids themselves. They'll vote. They'll build a country. Or unbuild it.

How in the world did the Education Establishment create this brave new child? In fact, there are four steps, which can be quickly described:

First, every school has to discard as much information as possible, using whatever pretext is handy. Some facts are not relevant; some are not multicultural; some are politically incorrect; some facts are too difficult for a particular group. It doesn't matter how you do it. The goal is that everything be thinned until finally you turn chunky beef soup into watery gruel. All the facts taught anywhere in the entire school should not fill up a small booklet. Now you're talking.

Second, insist for a hundred reasons that kids not be expected to remember or retain any of this thin fare. Rote memorization is laughed at. Drill and kill is scorned. Teaching to a test is attacked. So, there is little in the school to start with, and little of that ends up in a child's head.

Third, create easy, preferably subjective tests so that almost everyone gets an A or a B. These good grades suggest that children are mastering a great deal of knowledge. Parents are charmed by all the success. Nowadays educators are coming up with even more devious forms of testing, such as scrapbooks, peer review, and authentic assessment. The drift is away from expecting children to actually know anything specifically. Feelings and opinions are quite enough. Explaining how you approach the problem is praised. Correct answers are frowned upon.

Four, everything in the school and in the classroom must be enveloped in a smog of important-sounding, newfangled methods: Constructivism, Self-Esteem, Cooperative Learning, Critical Thinking, National Standards, 21st Century Learning, and dozens more. Gobbledegook is made flesh. Apparent activity is all-important. In many respects the school is theater, show biz, mime. Teachers pretend to teach; students pretend to learn. At the end of the process, the children know nothing.

Everything that occurs in school is like a dream you had last

night or the night before. Surely some interesting things happened. But you can't say exactly what. It's all very hazy now. Then even the memory of having a dream is gone. *Rasa.*

More evilly, what might actually be possible, and even easily achieved, is lost on the wind. In a world where everyone walks with a limp, running is no longer imaginable.

And so children, as never before in history, are turned into eunuchs of the mind. To the degree the Education Establishment can pull it off, children remain knowledge virgins. They are not unhappy. It's all they've ever known, these strangers in a strange land.

———

What Do Educators Mean When They Say "Education"?

One word. Two different worlds. No wonder so little genuine communication—or progress—occurs in education.

I had been writing about education for more than 20 years when I finally realized the divide, the scam, the silent sophistry, call it what you will, that renders so many discussions about education close to pointless.

When most people say the word "education," they mean something very specific, and almost everyone knows exactly what it is: reading, writing, arithmetic, geography, to be followed by history, science, literature, and the arts.

Now, if everyone in the discussion has this meaning in mind, they might build better schools together.

Unfortunately, the people who control public education and shape the debate have another meaning in their minds, and they know exactly what it is: social engineering, indoctrination, political correctness, and left-wing politics.

Now you see the problem and the point at which the game begins. Parents want one thing, i.e., Education! The Education Establishment wants to provide something else entirely, i.e., Education!

In truth, almost no understanding or agreement can occur. The parents don't know this. But the Education Establishment knows it very well, and must try to seduce and sedate the public without any intention of revealing what is really going on or what the stakes are.

Throughout the 20th century, the definitive rule that philosophers insisted on was: *define your terms.* But somehow in the perverse province of education, virtually nobody was encouraged to define their terms. So what we seem to have had was millions of words exchanged in a sort of semantic whiteout. Language and logic were soft and shapeless. As a result, the Education Establishment could promise to deliver what the public wanted, without ever intending to deliver it.

Parents heard all this high-minded talk about Education with a capital E: the worth of Education, the glory of Education, the urgent need to spend untold billions on Education. Who could guess that all this pretty verbiage was actually saying: *we would like to control your children and make them behave as we think best; that's what we mean by "education."*

It's only when you finally grasp that the Education Establishment lives in an alternative universe, both verbally and philosophically, indeed, a generally hostile universe, that all their counter-productive strategies and bad results begin to make a strange kind of sense.

Make a list of the pedagogical fads of the 20th century. This list will run to more than 50 items, for example, Constructivism, Multiculturalism, Bilingual Education, Open Classroom, Relevance, Child Centered Education, etc., etc. Typically, each of these ideas is vigorously praised and promoted for a number of years; and then discovered to be a failure. The key point is, they were not intended to teach a particular subject, i.e., the service that parents wanted. Instead, they were designed more as marketing ploys, as Bold New Ideas, that the public would find appealing (compare today's 21st Century Skills). But the closer we look at the actual results, the more it's clear that each one was, all along, a device, a strategy, that serves the wrong kind of "education."

There is the crux of the matter. These methods and gimmicks do "good" only in that alternative universe focused on indoctrination and political correctness. They are not designed to do good in the world that most people live in.

Here's a way to rephrase all of this: the Education Establishment set up an elaborate and pretentious machinery to provide a range of products and services that the public never asked for. If you wish to improve the public schools, first, disable or ignore this machinery. Second, stand firmly in the semantic divide and tell these people: don't talk about "education" because for you this is just a propaganda term, a cover-up word. Instead, tell us what you are going to do specifically about reading, writing, arithmetic, geography, history, science, literature, and the arts.

When the Education Establishment means by "education" what we the people mean by "education," then we'll get somewhere.

———

Public Schools Are Worse Than Most People Believe
(And Have Been for Far Longer Than Most People Realize)

Most Americans hardly grasp how bad the public schools are. The Education Establishment has done a brilliant job at propaganda and deception. They have tried to deceive the public; and the public is deceived. Unfortunately. So here are several quotes from some of the smartest, most successful people in the USA, people you should trust completely. And they are saying that educationally speaking we are now having a near-death experience:

"When I compare our schools to what I see when I'm traveling abroad, I'm terrified for our workforce of tomorrow." Bill Gates, founder, Microsoft Corp.

"If companies were run like many education systems, they wouldn't last a week." Thomas Donohue, president, US Chamber of Commerce

"Will America lead… and reap the rewards? Or will we surrender that advantage to other countries with clearer vision?" Susan Hockfield, President, MIT

"Our record at fixing our K-12 education system is virtually unblemished by success." Norman Augustine, former CEO of Lockheed Martin

"If you don't solve (the K-12 education problem), nothing else is going to matter all that much." Alan Greenspan, former Chairman,

Federal Reserve

Scared? You should be.

Furthermore, the public seems to have no idea that the sabotage of the public schools (and thus our economy) was started long ago, 100 years or more. All the wonderful new methods discussed in your daily paper are the same old dreck from your grandparents' day. The ideas were bad then, and still are today. (Typically, progressive ideas stress sociological and psychological abstractions, but there's no mention of actually learning anything. So-called educators actually say such nonsense as, "It's not important that children know historical facts as long as they can think historically.")

Probably John Dewey's quote from 1898 sums up the assault best: "I believe that we violate the child's nature and render difficult the best ethical results, by introducing the child too abruptly to a number of special studies, of reading, writing, geography, etc., out of relation to this social life." That is, don't teach them anything.

I've recently read a book called *So Little For The Mind* by a Canadian academic writing in 1953 (Canada being entirely under the spell of American ideas). This brilliant author, Professor Hilda Neatby, tells us how barren the educational landscape already was sixty years ago:

"The faith of our experts is not faith in the ability of all to solve problems but the reverse. The material which would enable the individual to work out his own salvation is practically withheld in order that he may be more receptive to the ready-made solutions that are handed out.

"Probably many Canadian parents would at least understand the attitude of the man who said, 'Nowadays the school seems to be doing the job of the homes, and the home has to do the job the school was supposed to do. They spend their time teaching my son to wash his face; when he comes home I have to teach him to read and write.'

"For all his talk of democracy, the educator is generally authoritarian and dogmatic. Teacher-training institutions in general exist to indoctrinate; their task is not to discover truth, but to convey 'the truth.'...[Students complain] that whatever lip service may be paid to them, 'logical self-expression, problem solving, and creative thinking' are the very last things the college wants to develop in its students.

"The official attitude towards examinations is in accordance with the general feeling on which we have remarked that the use of the intellect is a painful thing, which people ought to be spared on humanitarian grounds.

"Whereas in the elementary school the child learned critical thinking, and in the junior high school, critical and independent thinking, in the senior high school he learns critical reflective thinking." (That's sarcasm, of course. Today, every day, we hear chatter about critical thinking. Look how far Canada had taken the same racket 60 years ago.)

All the dopey ideas that progressive educators unloosed upon kids circa 1950 are still the latest thing today. Our so-called experts have merely adopted new names and terms, new propaganda and PR. True story: schools got ever dumber, the public was robbed in plain sight.

Many people are in despair and say the public schools cannot possibly be saved. Bruce Smartt in his book *The Harsh Truth About Public Schools* states his thesis that everyone should homeschool their kids, that public schools are a hopeless brew of left-wing politics and raw greed. People influenced by Smartt say we should shut down the public schools. I'm not saying it's a bad idea; I just don't see this happening. So what are we to do?

One reason for optimism is that even the people inside education must know how rotten it is. These phonies have created an illiteracy crisis and tens of millions of students who never master basic math (such as fractions and decimals). How do   these pretenders live with their failures?

My hope is that more people get involved, get informed, and get indignant. Find out why Sight-Words don't work, Constructivism is nonsense, and New/Reform Math are hoaxes. You'll never trust the Education Establishment again. That's when we're going to see progress.

––––––

A Speech to Teenagers About Education

"Ladies and gentlemen... This will be a short speech about education. *Your education.* The bottom line is that you must take responsibility for it.

"Many of you already know that you have to take charge of your hair and your clothes. Perhaps you know that all too well. You're also figuring out that you have to take charge of your diet and exercise, of trying to look good and feel good. And you're figuring out you have to make some tough choices about how you spend your time and whom you spend it with. But some of you may not have figured out the education part. One reason is that there tends to be an adversarial relationship between schools and students. The tendency is to resist what adults want, to say, don't bother me with that serious stuff now. I'll worry about that in a few years.

"My suggestion is to start worrying today. Now!

"The main thing you might not have figured out is that a lot of people don't give a damn whether you become educated or not. Some of these people run the schools you go to. Some of you can't read well, and I guarantee that is the fault of the school. Some of you can't multiply and divide, and I guarantee that is the fault of the school. Some of you don't know where the Pilgrims came from, which direction they went in, or where they landed when they got there. Some of you don't know the names of the oceans, the freezing point of water, or what 8 times 8 is. And I guarantee that all this is the fault of the school. Some of you don't know the most basic things that any second-grader can understand and learn. Why don't you know these things? I guarantee it's the fault of the school.

"See what you're up against??

"When we study American schools, we see a lot of make-believe, of keeping kids busy and making it appear that they are being educated. They are not. You're not! Schools used to push students toward excellence. Now they'll let you drop like a stone toward mediocrity, if you let them.

"I think it's fair to say that American education has been warped by ideology and politics. What's that mean? Some people are all too willing to dumb you down so they can keep you in your place. Say no! Say to hell with you, buddy—I want to know more. I want to be educated. I want to be able to make intelligent choices. I want to be a good voter. I want to succeed if I go on to college. I want to be a smart educated parent when the time comes. I want to be able to help make this a better country.

"So, as I say, take control of your education. Learn what you have to learn; and keep right on going. Any time you see a word you don't know, look it up. Any time you see a name or a subject you haven't heard about, run to the nearest encyclopedia or search the web. Try to read at least one magazine cover to cover every week. Read a book a month. Go on offense. Take a look at the subjects you know and plan how you can extend that knowledge. Consider the subjects you know little about and figure the easiest way to move toward learning more. Take charge.

"Has this little pep talk been gloomy? That's because I find myself worrying about education stats. Did you know that this country has 50 million functional illiterates; that SAT scores are dropping; that our A students can't compete against the A students from other countries; that reporters go out on the street and find apparently ordinary citizens who don't know which way is north?...I just want to impress on you that in education, much more than you might realize, you are on your own. If you don't do it, it may not happen.

"Thomas Jefferson said we can't be ignorant and free at the same time. Ignorance is a kind of slavery. That has always been true. What's new is the number of people who might be pushing you in the wrong direction.

"I hope you'll push back with all your strength."

2. READING WARS

Why do we have 50,000,000 functional illiterates? Somebody must want that outcome.

Education Has Been Battered by Bad Faith

The easiest way to understand the field of education is to consider a legal concept: *bad faith*. It's been around for thousands of years; in Latin, the phrase was *mala fides*. Any time there's a split between what is claimed and what is fact, you've got bad faith.

Education is a field clearly disfigured by counterintuitive behavior crying out for explanation and cure. Why are our statistics and test scores so low, why do we have so many functional illiterates, why must we import so many of our scientists and engineers, and why do we have so many people at the college level who know very little? These are inexplicable mysteries until you factor in bad faith. Then everything makes sense.

Think of young teachers, fresh from ed school, teaching their first year of classes. These teachers have embraced the theories and methods taught to them. No matter how bad these approaches might be, the young teachers believe in them and are therefore acting in good faith.

But what about the professors at the ed schools? They're probably in their forties or fifties. They've been watching dismal results come back from the public schools for decades. They know that many popular fads are disasters. Most of these professors have heard of better ideas used in private schools, homeschooling, or other countries. But they keep promoting the same destructive ideas in the schools, with a reckless disregard of the damage caused.

Reading, the quintessential skill, provides a well-documented, open-and-shut case of bad faith lasting 85 years.

In the Roaring Twenties, the Education Establishment did research on what would be called Look and Say. Dr. Samuel Orton, a neurologist, conducted a study of reading difficulties. It was not his main field, and he was uncomfortable when he found himself at odds with the oncoming orthodoxy. However, in 1928 he published an article (in the *Journal of Educational Psychology*) titled "The 'Sight Reading' Method of Teaching Reading, as a Source of Reading Disability."

Dr. Orton reported on a "**group of children for whom, as I think we can show, this technique is not only not adapted but often proves an actual obstacle to reading progress, and moreover I believe that this group is one of considerable educational importance both because of its size and because here faulty teaching methods may not only prevent the acquisition of academic education by children of average capacity but may also give rise to far reaching damage to their emotional life.**"

This famously diffident quote says that Look-say will keep kids from reading *and* scramble their brains. Almost everyone in the field of reading at the professorial level would know this article. But in 1931, as the Depression reached its full fury, our left-wing educators jumped at the chance to impose this faulty method on the public schools of America, with disastrous results.

Fast-forward twenty years. The illiteracy crisis in the United States is obvious to everyone. This was the context in which Rudolf Flesch published *Why Johnny Can't Read* in 1955, a book that sold 8 million copies. It explains why we had an illiteracy problem (Sight-Words) and what to do about it (bring back phonics).

Instead, the Education Establishment doubled down on its discredited methods, forming the International Reading Association. This professional association had the tasks of destroying Flesch and imposing Sight-Words forever.

The point is that at two distinct points, everyone at the top of American education knew that Sight-Words didn't work, and in both cases, they went right on. Cut to the present, when we have 50 million functional illiterates and generally low literacy standards. Professors of education know that their methods hurt children. They know that slowly memorizing hundreds of Sight-Words is a horribly difficult task, which typically leads nowhere.

So we have eight decades of bad faith in the field of reading. Had we world enough and time, we could look at all the major theories, and you would see the same pattern. The Education Establishment favors the theories and methods that lead to bad results, and this is most blatantly so in reading. Bad faith followed by more bad faith.

But why? The short answer, I believe, is because John Dewey and his followers were far-left ideologues. They thought leveling was a good plan.

Progressive educators want to outwit nature and make everybody end up with similar IQs. Predictably, our schools will be a bust as schools. As indoctrination centers, they are successful.

But the educators are not calling the schools indoctrination centers; they are calling them places of education. And there is all the bad faith you need to kill a civilization.

ADDENDUM: Re: 50,000,000. The Department of Education claims that 32,000,000 adults in the US can't read. Another group just as large reads in a limited way—for example, at a third, fifth or seventh grade level. If "literate" is defined as "able to enjoy a good book," then the 50 million number is too low. Another study claims that 45% of American adults can't understand the labels on their pills. That would be at least 100 million stunted readers. Count it up any way you want, we have an illiteracy crisis in America. Thank the public schools.

ADDENDUM 2: Re: consistency. Everyone in education capitalizes many of the key terms in different ways, often in the same article. For example, we see sight words, sight-words, Sight Words, Sight-Words, etc. There is no point in pretending there is a perfect answer. Personally, I like to capitalize the main theories, such as Constructivism and Whole Word. I like to capitalize Sight-Words because they are an important problem.

———

There Are Two Americas... And One of Them Can't Read

Okay, folks, place your bets. Was it clueless incompetence on a cosmic scale? Or, was it John Dewey's collectivist wet dream turned Clockwork Orange?

One of these ways or the other, we became a country

with millions of people who can't read a cereal box, never mind instructions on a pill bottle when that exact skill might save a life. Prisons are full of people who can't read. The country's schools wallow in mediocrity. All thanks to educational malfeasance, decade after decade.

J'accuse! J'accuse! The so-called experts in charge of reading are derelict and destructive. Please, remove these parasites from our weary carcass.

Reading was always something that children learned, almost automatically, in the first few years of schools. They learn the alphabet, then A is for Apple, then the sounds of the letters, and soon everyone is reading.

John Dewey, however, opined that a concern with literature constituted "a perversion." Takes one to know one, John. This character actually lamented that children might sit alone enjoying a good book. He and his cronies seem to have set out to make sure it can't happen. I never know what to call these people. Quacks is accurate; but I prefer shameless hussies.

Now, let's focus on what children should be doing and on what timetable. We need at this point a few expert testimonies to establish a baseline.

One of our best-known educators is Marva Collins (1936-2015). She had this assertion on her website: "Children as young as 4 years of age are admitted to my school, at the beginning of every school year in September. I guarantee that they will ALL be reading by Christmas, three months later. That has been the results since I started my school in 1975." Note that the lady says: "ALL," even as some public schools casually accept that one-fifth of their students might need to be classified as dyslexic.

Sibyl Terman and Charles Walcutt said in *Reading: Chaos and Cure* (1958) that: "Most of the children in America could be taught to read in a few weeks or months at the age of five."

Mona McNee and Alice Coleman, two of England's leading educators, both with 40+ years in the school trenches, state in their book *The Great Reading Disaster* (2007) that: **"All children, apart from the blind, profoundly deaf and brain damaged, can learn to read by the end of infant school [age seven]. Reading schemes should not go on forever and after two years children should be capable of choosing their own books."**

These quotes should bring tears to our eyes. They tell us what is normal, and how quickly the process moves along in sensible schools using proper methods.

Instead we have a totally lunatic situation where millions of children fall behind in elementary grades and never recover. They hate books, and their education remains in free fall. This is the predictable results wherever phonics is discarded and Whole Word (or Sight-Words) is imposed on children.

Here's another way to judge appropriate progress. You have probably learned a foreign language, or you know someone who did. This task might take a few years, at which point you're reading, writing and speaking a wholly different language from your own. Note that a whole new vocabulary must be learned. But give it two or three years, and you can manage.

The situation for American children in our public schools should be much easier. They are "native speakers" who show up on Day One knowing nearly 10,000 words and names. All these words and their pronunciations are ALREADY in the brains of the children. All they need is the tool kit that lets them recognize the words in print. This isn't a difficult thing to do, and experts tell us they can do it rather quickly.

How very dysfunctional our public schools have become! American children learning to read French make faster progress than American children learning to read English.

So let's think about this: our Education Establishment doesn't accomplish much of anything and they take many tedious years to do it. *Hmm*, you'd almost have to conclude that they're faking it, that they have no interest in teaching people to read. Why else would anyone use a loser pedagogy like Whole Word?

Just for a moment, consider the silly theory that our top educators put forward. There should be no sounding out of letters and syllables; instead, children should memorize words as graphic designs or diagrams. Put yourself in the head of a kid showing up for first grade. The teacher points to a design like "**xhyld**" and instructs, "This means house. When you see this, say *house*." So, can you memorize "**xhyld**"?

Probably. But will you be able to pick it out from similar designs, of which there are dozens, such as: **xhydd, xyhld, xhydl, xyyld, xhdyl, xyjkl, xkyht, xygld,** etc. of course, you'll need to be ready for variations such as **XHYDD, XYHLD, XHYDL, XYYLD, XHDYL, XYJKL, XKYHH, XYGLD**. Okay, maybe you have a photographic memory, so you might have a chance. But no ordinary person has even a tiny chance of being literate. You can probably feel the dyslexia creeping into your brain.

And you've just started on your first list of words. You'll need 5,000 words to be barely literate. But guess what the guru of this madcap theory said? "Children can acquire sight vocabularies of 50,000 words." Not without a chip implant. But it's even worse. College students probably need 100,000 words. (Total English vocabulary is over 500,000 words.)

The idea that reading has something to do with memorizing word-shapes is nuts. There's no polite way to say it. English is a phonetic language, and you first need to learn the alphabet and then the sounds they represent.

(Just for fun, let's jump back in history 50 centuries, to that bright day when a genius with super-hearing announced to a friend. "Know what? I can write down our entire language with about 25 symbols."

The friend naturally said, "*You are crazy*. We've got thousands and thousands of words."

The First Writer explained, "No, it's easy. Here's how it works. Take the word *bat*. So I write a b-sound, an a-sound and a t-sound, thus: B-A-T. Now, say that back to me fast."

Whereupon the friend said, "*Ba...ah...tuh....*BAT! Darn, it works! How the heck did you figure that out?" And at that moment the friend became the First Reader.

Note that the processes are complements. Reading and writing are the reverse of each other, like ice into water, and back again. We seem to be wired to do both processes with amazing speed. Sounds become letters; letters become sounds.)

The Whole Word frauds say: *But English has so many inconsistencies.* Well, it certainly has some. But remember, kids don't care because they ALREADY know the pronunciations.

Really, it's quite possible to read phonetically without knowing all the rules and details. (I'm Exhibit A for this.) Similarly, most English speakers do quite well despite not being able, for example, to conjugate common but very inconsistent verbs, such as "to be.")

So let's say kids go down the formal phonics route, and do memorize 100 rules. That's a walk in the park next to memorizing 100,000 words. This has always been the single most demented aspect of Whole Word, that learning 100 rules and exceptions is

said to be too much work, but memorizing 100,000 sight-words is
something any child can do.

I'm not keen on memorizing little rules myself. I've worried about
this aspect. But I've been comforted by Mona McNee's conclusion
that children love all the little rules. It's like a game or a puzzle for
them. As they gain mastery, they feel better about themselves and more
enthusiastic about reading. Sounds good to me.

Joan Dunn, a teacher, wrote in 1955: "**The children... want to be
taught step by step, so that they can see their progress. The duller
they are, the more important and immediate is this need.**" All of
my research suggests that Dunn's second sentence is education's Big
Profundity. The slower kids are simply being destroyed because the
schools refuse to teach the basics in a systematic way.

Samuel Blumenfeld (1927-2015) provides the bottom line for
the whole society: "In fact, most reading problems can be avoided by
teaching a child phonics at home before he or she goes to school."

Inoculate your children. Teach them to read early.

———

News for Educators: Guessing Is Not Reading

If a teacher tells a child to guess what a word is, that teacher is
basically saying: "I'm not going to teach you how to read. I don't care if
you learn to read. You will probably become a functional illiterate and
that's okay with me."

Admittedly, many teachers are in a hammer lock, as superintendents
and principals may have ordered the teachers to use an unworkable
pedagogy or be fired.

So I'm not saying the teacher is thinking those thoughts consciously.
I'm saying it's AS IF the teacher were thinking those thoughts. The
children end up in the same place no matter how you slice it. For a very
simple reason: guessing is NOT reading.

Reading is processing letters into sounds, from left to right. You
don't study the words as if they are logos or faces. You don't look
around the whole paragraph. You don't analyze the illustrations. You
don't think of what you might know about the subject. You don't try to

deduce meaning from context. All that is blather and bogus.

Reading involves a very simple skill: you read the words. That is, you convert them into the sounds that the letters represent. As I say, you READ the words. You absolutely do not guess the words. That is the opposite of reading. It is anti-reading.

We are discussing one of the most astonishing hoaxes of the 20th century. The Education Establishment convinced itself (so they claim), and then tried to convince the nation, that the average person could memorize tens of thousands of words as graphic designs. Well, as you know from trying to name a celebrity or a famous painting, and the name escapes you for a minute, naming designs of any kind can sometimes be very tricky. So the official experts had to come up with various crutches. Use context. Study the pictures. Guess!

of course, if a child does not in fact know how to read, that child has NO CHOICE but to guess. If you are in Shanghai, walking down a street where the signs are written in Chinese, you will use every trick in the book to guess what those symbols might mean. You might think: well, this looks like a place where busses stop, I'll wait here for a bus. You might be right. Or the sign might say: LOADING ZONE.

If you could actually read Chinese, you wouldn't guess, you would know.   Can't read Chinese? of course you have to guess. You have to be very clever. You may get a few right; but you will experience a lot of frustration, waste a lot of time and energy, and often be wrong.

That's a perfect description of what happens to the victims of Whole Word in our public schools.

Now, if you are smart enough to be reading this article, you probably could memorize a few thousand Sight-Words. Some very smart people actually go to college and read using the techniques mandated by Whole Word. Typically, these people have headaches; they're anxious and uncomfortable; they don't read for pleasure. So, yes, there is a tiny minority of brainy people who can read, however tensely, with Sight-Words. You may be one of them, so you might be thinking: *What's the big deal? I think I could do that.*

Please put that thought out of your head. That thought is one of the big reasons why the frauds running our educational system could get away with their nonsense for all these decades. To put it bluntly: the smarter citizens are busy preening while the dumber citizens are pushed further down.

You are probably in the top few percent of the population,

intelligence-wise. Let's look at the people in the middle; they are lucky to get over 500 Sight-Words. Let's look at the bottom 30%; some of these kids cannot learn 100 Sight-Words, even after years of trying. Meanwhile, the rest of their education is on hold. Next thing they know, they're in middle school and as miserable as drowning cats. Predictably, they start showing signs of ADHD. They are given Ritalin. Parents are told their kids are dyslexic and they'll never read because of something wrong with their brains. The whole thing is a nightmare—an unnecessary nightmare.

So don't suppose that because you could learn some Sight-Words, that therefore little Johnny Doe, with an IQ of 100, can do anything close. No, he is simply depressed, and dreaming of the day he can drop out of school and take up a life of crime. In so far as you support Whole Word in the public schools, you abet that destruction.

All of this craziness is contained in that one word: guessing. Major theoreticians (all of these are people with Ph.D.'s in Education) stated flat-out that when children encounter a word they don't know, they should guess or skip it.

For the average child, this pedagogy is death. Your life as a student is over. You can be a worker of some kind, but probably a low-level one. Meanwhile, there are jobs and accomplishments that will be forever out of your reach, but they may have been easy for you if you had only learned to read.

Correct that: if only your school had bothered to teach you to read.

CODA: I have a reason for writing this strongly worded article. I don't think we can trust the people who came up with Guessing Is Reading. Nor can we trust many of the other weird things these alleged experts come up with. Fact is, we could've done much better throughout the 20th century. Now we've gone into the 21st century on the wrong foot. But here's good news: there is so much room for improvement. Why, just imagine what would happen if schools actually start teaching again.

———

How Children Learn to Read: A Primer For Teachers And Parents

The Reading Wars, astonishingly enough, continue to rage. Rudolf Flesch explained the problem in 1955, in his famous book titled *Why Johnny Can't Read*.

Many other smart people have explained the problem again and again. But still our schools persist in using precisely the bad methods that Flesch discredited.

In particular, the schools make children memorize words as shapes (a.k.a. Sight-Words). This practice is the single main reason why we have so many functional illiterates. Bottom line: get rid of Sight-Words, use some version of phonics, and children usually learn to read by the age of seven. Instead, many public schools hang on to ideas that cause reading failure. It's important to understand WHY these ideas don't work.

There are two ways for a child to "read" a word: sound it out (that is, say it or pronounce it). Or, name it as a visual object, just as a child might name a make of car. For decades, public schools insisted on the naming of shapes, which virtually precludes literacy. Now, as part of the strategic retreat known as Balanced Literacy, many schools dogmatically insist that the two methods be taught simultaneously. This is better but still only half-way back from hell. The student's brain will continually flip-flop from one mode to the other. So the student will be a tense, confused reader.

Here is the sort of bizarre comments you see ad infinitum on the Internet: "One of the most precarious dangers in this realm is the assumption that there is one way to teach reading... I teach a strong phonics based curriculum, but we also teach 20 new sight-words every 2 weeks." Unbelievable. That means her students are supposed to memorize 300+ Sight-Words for the year. Virtually no child can achieve mastery of that many Sight-Words. Even if they do, they'll be hopelessly schizophrenic for the rest of their reading careers. What a mess. Let's zoom in on the actual process and try to see the sins as they occur.

Imagine a child reading this sentence: "The bird saw a...." When the child's eyes move toward the next word, what happens?? If the word is processed LEFT TO RIGHT AS SOUNDS, that is real reading. However, if the eyes scan BACK AND FORTH over the whole shape (which is how we look at a car), as the brain struggles to recall its name, that's Sight-Word reading and a guarantee of low literacy.

Freeze the frame. Note that the instant the eyes start backward (that is, leftward) is the instant you have inefficient reading. Clearly, the eyes are covering the same ground two or three times. Isn't this obvious, even to professors of education? Reading should be a steady left-to-right, 1-2-3-4 process. Much like playing the piano, where you don't go back and play previous notes; much like walking along a sidewalk, where you don't suddenly walk backward; much like talking to a friend, where you don't start speaking the unfolding sentence in reverse.

Reading, for most people, means you are covering a few hundred words a minute. Even a slow reader is reading two words a second! To keep this pace, there can be no hesitation, no going back, no retracing one's steps. You just bound along, sort of like a boy running across a stream from one stone to the next. Sometimes you might go back and make sure that the words said what you think they said. But ordinary reading, of a novel or a magazine, is a very fast—let us say, relentless—activity, always moving forward.

Sight-Word reading, precisely because it trains the eyes to scan UP and DOWN, RIGHT to LEFT, and LEFT to RIGHT, is the death of reading. The loons pushing this thing claim that kids can identify a word at a glance. Yes, this can happen if we're talking about the Nike swoosh, the American flag, or a STOP sign, anything very distinctive that you've seen dozens of times. But for every Sight-Word the child knows with automaticity, there are 5 more the child knows with only partial-automaticity and then there are 10 other words that have not yet been dealt with. It's basically like a child trying to run across the stream on a series of rocks, half of which are under water or covered with slime. The runner won't make it.

Now, let's move ahead one-half second and freeze the frame again. "The bird saw a xzgk." *Uh-oh*, the child doesn't know the word *xzgk*. With a nervous twitch, his eyes jump ahead looking for a familiar word. This is the essential act in a method called "context clues." The child, not able to read properly, is supposed to examine surrounding words (or pictures) to figure out an unknown word. Now he goes back and starts the sentence again and reads up to the unfamiliar word, still doesn't know it, and lurches ahead to the next sentence, then to a sentence after that, and then comes back. On the simplest mechanical level, you can see how many extra tracks and arabesque the eyes will execute.

As a practical matter, an educated adult can sometimes use context to deduce an unknown word. But this works only if you know virtually all the other words on the page, and you have a lot of background knowledge. To tell a child to use this technique is the height of quackery. But that's precisely what our Education Establishment has been doing for 75 years.

The young reader, far from knowing most of the words on the page, may only know half of them. Can you imagine the panic and confusion as this child searches ahead for a known entity? The child's eyes may move backward as often as forward. So you have a huge amount of wasted energy and wasted time, all because the child cannot actually read.

To reinforce the total insanity of this gimmick called context clues, let's consider this sentence: "The man walked into a xwygq."

Even if we confine ourselves to five letter words (a Sight-Word reader would no doubt include four- and six-letter words among his guesses), you have dozens of possibilities. There may be many pages of text where you would never be able to determine the missing word; or you may be able to determine it approximately but only after minutes of wasted effort.

(By the way, what is *xwygq*? Did the man walk into a motel or a hotel? Did he walk into a field? Or a ditch, drain or sewer? Perhaps he walked into a truck, train, or wagon. No? What about a house or a store? He could walk into a fight, couldn't he? A storm? Ah, I got it! He walked into a fence. What a fool. But not as big a fool as someone who teaches little children to use context clues to guess at mystery words. As opposed to teaching the child to read those words.)

I think you can devastate the case for Sight-Word in many separate ways: 1) by pointing out that English has far too many words for someone to remember even a fraction of the important ones; 2) far too many similar word-shapes for the brain to quickly distinguish, for example, **right, fright, bright, sight, fight, light, tights, mighty, flighty; nightly,** etc.; 3) far too many different cases and typefaces, which means that any given word-shape is never fixed but likely to appear in a chaos of alternative forms. All of these variables place tremendous (indeed, impossible) demands on memory. Sight-Words, at the start, may have been someone's sincere theory; but it quickly degenerated into a vicious hoax. Even if a child wanted to memorize a large number of Sight-Words, there would have to be relentless drawing of these word-designs and endless flash-card drills, the most brutally repetitive work you can imagine. All of which our Education Establishment forbids!

So we hardly need, you might think, still another reason to dismiss Whole Word. But public schools keep pushing this flop, shamefully enough; and kids are being damaged. So this point is intended to be the clincher. Simply visualize for yourself what a child's eyes are actually doing. If they move steadily to the right across the page, that's reading. If they're roaming around, searching ahead, or backtracking, that's not reading. That's a dog looking frantically for a buried bone. Case closed.

Certainly if a person could memorize tens of thousands of English word-shapes and name them with perfect automaticity, well, that's successful sight-reading. That's what some disingenuous educators claim can happen routinely. But all the evidence says this happy picture rarely occurs. Most children top out below 500 and become effectively illiterate. Mastering even 2000 Sight-words is a huge accomplishment. (There are super-brains that reach 4,000 and actually go through college reading that way, but they always report how nervous, tense, and miserable they are.)

Meanwhile, the average kids have been chewed up and spat on the ground. To them, a typical newspaper story looks like this: "Senator John xxxxx joked that he never xxxx that he could xxxx so much. His wife xxxxx, 'John's like a xxxx.' They xxxx loudly and xxxxxx their xxxxx." To guess even one of those mystery words would be quite an achievement.

Here's another sick part. You could construct a test, with multiple choice answers, to measure comprehension. With some lucky guesses, a kid might pass. The school might actually state that the boy reads at "near grade-level" or some such. In this way the schools cover up the magnitude of the tragedy. And so it continues.

Can a child actually read? It's so easy to find out. Hand the child a newspaper and say, "Read this paragraph." If the child leaves out words, replaces words, guesses wildly, or reverses words, you know the child can't read. Blame the school.

———

Reading Is Easy. (Illiteracy Is Hard)

This country, for the last 80 years, has been living through what future historians might call the Great American Reading Swindle. The experts claimed to believe in a method that didn't work. In order to protect it, and to shield themselves from charges of educational misconduct, they generated endless shock waves of intellectual disorientation.

Here is jargon concocted by our elite experts during this long national nightmare: **psycholinguistics, miscue analysis, reading strategies, comprehension strategies, whole word, guessing, picture reading, whole language, sight-words, balanced literacy, reading readiness, word walls, active learning practices, closed instructional activities, high-frequency words, thinking and learning about print, invented spelling, reading recovery, emergent literacy, creative curriculum approach, functional systemic linguistic theory, rich literacy activities, authoring cycle, capability beliefs, post-reading, lifelong reader, cognitive flexibility theory, independent reading, kid watching,** etc.

The drift of all this malarkey is that reading is a very difficult thing to do. The Education Establishment needed to keep this self-serving idea in play because they couldn't seem to teach kids to read. After all, the experts would insist, it's so very hard to do! Don't blame us!

In fact, reading is easy to do, and to teach. Consider what these famous reading experts have to say:

Grace Fernald (*Remedial Techniques in Basic School Subjects*, 1943): "Since no abilities are required for the mastery of reading, writing, and arithmetic which are not already possessed by the ordinary, normal individual, it seems obvious that there is no such thing as a person of normal intelligence who cannot learn these basic skills."

Rudolf Flesch (*Why Johnny Can't Read*, 1955): "We could have perfect readers in all schools in the second grade if we taught our children [correctly]... It's very simple. Reading means getting meaning from certain combinations of letters. Teach a child what each letter stands for and he can read. I know, you say, it can't be that simple. But it is."

Sibyl Terman and Charles Walcutt (*Reading: chaos and cure*, 1958): "It is absurdly easy to teach a child to read with the proper method…We shall tell you about various schools, now functioning, where a problem reader is virtually unheard of."

Samuel Blumenfeld (ca. 1990): "All children, except the very seriously impaired, develop their innate language faculty extremely rapidly from ages 2 to 6. In fact, by the time they are six they have developed speaking vocabularies in the thousands of words, and can speak with clarity and grammatical correctness without having had a single day of formal education. In other words, children are dynamos of language learning and can easily be taught to read between ages 5 and 7, provided they are taught in the proper alphabetic-phonics way."

Siegfried Engelmann (*War against the schools' academic child abuse*, 1992): "I have never seen a kid with an IQ of over 80 that could not be taught to read in a timely manner (one school year), and I've worked directly or indirectly (as a trainer) with thousands of them. I've never seen a kid that could not be taught arithmetic and language skills."

Don Potter (2012): "The secret of making learning to read easy for children is not to confuse them at the very beginning. Children who learn the alphabet letter names and are taught to read from the sounds represented by the letters will have a very easy time learning to read. (To mention just a few of the very fine programs that are available, I would put Blumenfeld's *Alpha-Phonics* near the head of list, Dolores Hiskes' *Phonics Pathways* is an exemplary phonics program, Rudolf Flesch's *Exercises* in his *Johnny* work for me every time, and Hazel Loring's *Reading Made Easy with Blend Phonics for First Grade* makes teaching reading a snap for any age student.)"

In order to make reading difficult, our Education Establishment embraced every wrongheaded theory they could find. They dwelled obsessively on problems, and on creating roadblocks. They concocted an array of alibis and sophistries to excuse their failure. Instead of emphasizing that English is at least 97% phonetic, they constantly lied that English is hardly phonetic at all.

Basically, phonetic reading is a vast mnemonic device, that is, there are many easy-to-remember rules to help you read. When you see a b-word (beach, bread, etc.), you know for sure it starts *buh-*. That eliminates more than 95% of the possibilities. Each subsequent letter eliminates more options, until you know the word exactly.

Conversely, suppose you're memorizing Sight-Words; and the next day you see a Sight-Word you're not sure you know. Naturally, you worry that you misremembered it in some way. How can you be certain? Your only sure recourse is to find somebody who can read!

Whole Word is quite a crime and a joke. All those diagrams can look more or less alike. Here's an easy way to experience what kids endure. Hold a book upside down in front of a mirror and try to read, in a normal left-to-right way, what you see in the mirror. Focus on smaller designs. Try to memorize one of them; then try to find that same design again. You'll probably see this process as annoyingly difficult. You'll probably feel dyslexia engulf your brain.

That's the essence of the Great American Reading Swindle.

One obvious deduction: people who would lie to you about reading, the one essential skill, would hardly hesitate to lie about the rest of the curriculum.

The Illiteracy Machine Wants Your Kids

Every attempt to improve education in this country will fail unless we first make sure that children can read. This goal, however, is impossible to reach, given that the Education Establishment aggressively obstructs our path.

Dysfunctional is the best way to describe the Education Establishment's official doctrine on reading. These methods are endlessly promoted; but they don't work.

The only hope is that parents by the millions understand how reading should be taught, so they can demand proper methods. This article tries to explain the basics in a few words.

English is a phonetic language and must be read phonetically. What does that mean? You see an "a" and you know to say "*ah*." That's it. Each letter signifies a sound (or a cluster of similar sounds). Soon you see "ha" and know to blend the two sounds and say "*ha*." You see "hat" and know to blend the three sounds and say "*hat*." It's a beautiful thing.

Millions of children can't read because they were not taught letters and sounds. Instead they were told to memorize entire words visually. As a hypothetical example, they are shown an object such as "*fjhq*" and told to say "bike." You are probably thinking: but that's completely arbitrary. Precisely! The Whole Word approach to reading means that all mnemonic clues are given up.

To a six-year-old, English words (or Sight-Words, as the educators call them) seem without logic or reason. That's the problem. Memorizing large numbers of arbitrary designs is an extremely difficult project.

Test yourself on these eight symbols: ^) % ~ # > " <. Memorize that they are pronounced: "This is not how we learn to read."

It's just eight symbols. Take a few hours. Write them down over and over. Do you think you'll reach the point where you can quickly read these symbols in a different order, for example: > " % ^ #) < ~

This test will probably seem awkward and difficult. Please wallow in those feelings of *helplessness*. Now you know the essence of what most children experience when they try to memorize their first 25 Sight-Words:

> the of and a to in is you that it he for was on
> are as with his they at be this from I have

Note there is no logic in the order, no story. There are no clues to suggest pronunciation. Many designs look almost alike. (Here's a shocker: teachers in third and fourth grades often report that some students still confuse "is" and "the.")

When the children are alone, they can read only what they have perfectly memorized. Remember, they don't know the alphabet and sounds. Children are trying to identify shapes or designs, much as we recognize pennies, dimes, nickels, and quarters at a glance. Children with exceptional visual memories can make progress. But the average child has a great deal of trouble with this. Slower children fail from the first weeks onward.

The Internet is full of professors and merchants enthusiastically extolling the glories of Sight-Words. Here is one version of the official doctrine:

"During preschool and the primary grades your child is building the foundations for a lifetime of reading. One of the building blocks of a strong foundation in reading is sight-words. The ability to easily identify and understand high-frequency words in texts helps the young reader move efficiently and effectively through reading tasks. While it is important for young readers to master

the core set of 220 high-frequency words by the end of third grade, this does not mean that sight-word instruction ends on the last day of the third grade school year. Sight-word instruction should be an important part of the fourth grade reading program as well…"

This is bizarre. You can tell from the low goals that this approach is tedious and slow. Even in the fourth grade the students will be readers only in a very limited sense. Clearly, they haven't been reading stories, geography, newspapers, real books, etc.

Now compare this glacial progress with systematic phonics, which generally allows first graders to read in less than six months. Read, that is, tens of thousands of English words.

Here is more of the cheerful hustle from our Education Establishment: **"Sight words free up a child's energy to tackle more challenging words. Reading is tough work! As fluent readers we often underestimate the amount of focus and energy reading takes when you don't know most of the words on the page before you."**

Typically, Sight-Words don't free up anything. Children search desperately in their memories for what each design might be. It never gets easier. The official doctrine actually tells kids to GUESS or SKIP AHEAD, which is what illiterate people necessarily do.

Of course, the brain always looks for easier ways to do things. After a delay of a few years, the more verbal children figure out the phonics inside the Sight-Words. (And most schools now teach some phonics mixed with the Sight-Words.) But the very process of memorizing Sight-Words undercuts the phonics reflex. There may be subtle impairments, often called dyslexia. This helps explain why we have so many millions of adults who can read to some degree but don't read for pleasure.

Almost half the children never do find the phonics. Those children become functionally illiterate, able to recognize roughly 100-1000 Sight-Words, logos, product names, street names, etc.

In summary, Phonics is a vast mnemonic device fairly easy to master. Whole Word, with no mnemonics, is a vast Illiteracy Machine. Why does the Education Establishment keep pushing this kid-killer? Are these people incompetent, greedy, subversive, sadistic, or what?

NOTE: children who have trouble reading can be classified as having special needs. Schools can receive funding from the government to deal with this problem. The school thereby has a perverse incentive *not* to do a good job. Sad to say, illiteracy and dyslexia are big businesses.

3. MATH WARS

**Students reach college not knowing what 6 x 8 is.
Could that happen by accident?**

One Thing We Know For Sure:
Our Education Establishment Hates Math

just heard it on the radio, a young boy complaining about how pathetically incompetent US kids are at math. Compared to kids from around the world, Americans are in the bottom 25%. Could it be that bad? Is our Education Establishment that gifted at non-teaching?

So what was the boy's proposed solution? You should buy a franchise for something called Mathnasium and teach the kids in your community how to do arithmetic. Because, as you know, the public schools can't manage this complex feat. I've got nothing for or against Mathnasium. But here's the bigger point: a remedial tutoring operation like this should NEVER be necessary. If public schools do a proper job, students learn math and don't need any outside help. I said IF.

Here's how one researcher summed up our dilemma: "Tests showed U.S. fourth-graders performing poorly, middle school students worse, and high school students are unable to compete... Chances are, even if your school compares well in SAT scores, it will still be a lightweight on an international scale."

Well, you don't need to be Einstein to conclude that our public schools don't have a clue about teaching arithmetic. Their greatest gift is selecting the worst methods and then claiming they are "research-based."

Since about 1990, public schools push something called Reform Math. But private and parochial schools don't use this rubbish. Especially homeschoolers don't. These are very picky consumers and squabble among themselves over the merits of Singapore Math, Saxon

Math, Math Mammoth, MathUSee, and other ingenious programs that actually teach math, which has to be a miracle because our Education Establishment can't pull it off.

Why not? Here's my guess: they don't want to. They're collectivists at heart and believe in leveling, which quickly leads to dumbing-down. I'll explain how this darkness works. But first a light moment. Here's how one wit summed up the last 60 years:

Teaching Math in the 1950s (Traditional): *A logger sells a load for $100. His production cost is 4/5 of the price. How much is his profit?*

Teaching Math in the 1970s (New Math): *A logger trades a set "L" (of lumber) for a set "M" (of money). The cardinality of set "M" is 100. The cardinality of subset "C" (his cost) is 20 less than "M." What is the cardinality of set "P" (his profit)?*

Teaching Math in the 1990s (Reform Math): *A logger sells a load for $100. Her production is $80 and her profit is $20. Your assignment: underline the number 20.*

My take is that New Math and Reform Math are the same long-running gimmick. Mix simple stuff with complex stuff and thereby create an impossible brew, counterintuitive, impossible to master, and virtually guaranteeing bad math scores. This brew—often called "fuzzy math"—is packaged into various curricula and textbooks, with clever names, pretty graphics, and fancy printing, all of which is lipstick on a large rat.

The so-called experts claim they are teaching concepts and understanding, which sounds impressive. But the kids never master simple arithmetic because basic, common-sense content and memorization are summarily omitted. New Math and Reform Math are based on the same false premise, that children need to study abstract concepts before they can do practical applications. **Exactly backward.**

Here is another image that might help some readers understand what our non-teachers are doing nowadays. Suppose you need to learn archery. And I teach you archery by explaining the history and concept of sports, of muscular activity, of competition, the need for eye-hand coordination, the need for being in shape. And every week I toss in some aspect of archery—"Look, this is an arrow," and next week,

"This is a bow." Meanwhile you're learning about football, baseball, basketball, and the concepts that each of these games is built on. What does it all mean? Other than that your teacher is crazy. It means you won't learn archery for many months. And your grasp of archery will be muddled in with bowling, softball hockey and skiing. But we all know there are only a few essential skills in archery: holding the bow, drawing the bow, aiming at a target. You have to focus on the basic skills and practice them with respect. You need to isolate them and master them. Learning arithmetic is exactly the same. You don't need to know the history of math to learn how to add 12 + 13. But the National Council of Teachers of Mathematics (NCTM) wants to pretend that the best way to learn arithmetic is the study of pre-algebra, pre-trig, set theory, and whatever else the cat drags in.

I recently reviewed two books on Amazon, both published around 1965, that were intended to explain New Math to parents and kids. These books are dense, unfriendly, chaotic, inappropriate, impossible to understand without repeated readings—exactly like New Math itself. Here's the good part. The country saw all these flaws immediately, and put New Math in the dumpster, where it belongs.

Never forget how dreadful New Math was. The smartest educators worked on this thing for years. They are incompetent or they are criminals. Either way, you know this well is poisoned.

I can't imagine that any human sincerely trying to teach arithmetic to children would devise New Math. I don't know how you could conclude that it's anything but a vicious hoax. (Conceptually, I would suggest that New Math is like Whole Word, which at that time was preventing millions of children from becoming fluent readers. Note that both gimmicks promised fluency but delivered disability.)

The next historical development is revealing. The mad scientists who created New Math went back to their laboratories for a decade and, instead of coming up with a single program as before, concocted a DOZEN programs. The strategy would seem to be: divide and confuse. Note: all programs were bad. The experts seem to have learned nothing about teaching math but a lot about overwhelming and bamboozling the public. Collectively, these dozen programs were called Reform Math. Students hated them. Parents hated them. Most teachers hated them. Typically, a community would waste years figuring out how much they hated a program; evaluating other programs; selecting the new program; only to find that everyone hated it, too. Some of the infamous names are *MathLand, Connected Math, TERC, Chicago Math, Everyday Math, Core-Plus, Constructivist Math*, and many more. Parents saw the continuity with New Math and derisively called the new curricula "New New Math."

Wikipedia rather cutely explains, "Traditional mathematics focuses on teaching algorithms that will lead to the correct answer." How quaint.

These new programs, on the other hand, emphasize all the bad ideas now ruining the teaching of most subjects. For example: **Cooperative Learning** makes kids work in teams so they never learn to think for themselves, the very thing you have to do in a serious test. **Constructivism** requires that children invent methods for themselves, so they never learn to do anything automatically, such that 30 years later, every restaurant check is a new challenge. **Self-Esteem** is stressed, so even if kids don't know anything, the teachers say that they do. One spectacularly destructive component is called **Spiraling** which requires that teachers jump from topic to topic *without requiring that students master any of them*. Are there any good ideas? Don't bet on it.

What grounds, you might protest, do I have for such cynicism? I have two words for you: New Math. This thing was rotten at its core; and everyone saw it. Years later, when the professors came back with the first wave of Reform Math, it was at bottom the same old goulash. Most of this new mischief was repudiated by subsequent tweaks. Which prove the experts learn little from any of their failures. These people will purvey bad to the degree they can get away with bad.

In fact, a tiny little anecdote in a small book written in 1953 shows us how long the anti-math plot has been in play. The book is titled *Retreat from Learning: Why Teachers Can't Teach*. The author is a young woman who taught in tough Brooklyn schools for several years before giving up; her name is Joan Dunn.

She writes: "...educators are still undecided about the best way to teach the alphabet. They go through agonies because two and two equal four and a way must be found to teach that disturbing fact without mentioning numbers. The poor grade-school teacher finds herself emptying gallons of water into pint containers because some educational theorist (who probably has not taught in 30 years) has decided that her little charges might be permanently scarred if exposed to the brutal fact that 2 + 2 equals 4."

I have to say I love the wit and wisdom of Joan Dunn. You see, this is many years before New Math was set loose upon the country. Clearly, however, all the counterproductive ideas were brewing in this Brooklyn public school by 1950. The so-called educators simply don't want to teach basic arithmetic. There is no way Joan Dunn could anticipate where all this nuttiness would go; but she glimpses the essence. The educators are squirming to find a way, any way whatsoever, to avoid teaching arithmetic. And that is what we are still seeing today, as the bad ideas already described, mutated into today's Common Core.

––––––

These programs are, I believe, perverse top to bottom. But that's not the end of the sin. To protect the foolishness, these programs present themselves to us in a whirlwind of numbing verbiage, technical mumbo-jumbo, and pseudoscientific pretension. Let's go to the National Council of Teachers of Math and read their breathless "Curriculum Focal Points":

"Children develop strategies for adding and subtracting whole numbers on the basis of their earlier work with small numbers. They use a variety of models, including discrete objects, length-based models (e.g., lengths of connecting cubes), and number lines, to model 'part-whole,' 'adding to,' 'taking away from,' and 'comparing' situations to develop an understanding of the meanings of addition and subtraction and strategies to solve such arithmetic problems. Children understand the connections between counting and the operations of addition and subtraction (e.g., adding two is the same as 'counting on' two). They use properties of addition (commutativity and associativity) to add whole numbers, and they create and use increasingly sophisticated strategies based on these properties (e.g., 'making tens') to solve addition and subtraction problems involving basic facts. By comparing a variety of solution strategies, children relate addition and subtraction as inverse operations."

And that, my friends, is what they do to First Graders.

Can you stand more? **"Students understand the meanings of multiplication and division of whole numbers through the use of representations (e.g., equal-sized groups, arrays, area models, and equal 'jumps' on number lines for multiplication, and successive subtraction, partitioning, and sharing for division). They use properties of addition and multiplication (e.g., commutativity, associativity, and the distributive property) to multiply whole**

numbers and apply increasingly sophisticated strategies based on these properties to solve multiplication and division problems involving basic facts. By comparing a variety of solution strategies, students relate multiplication and division as inverse operations."

That's your Third Graders, cannon fodder for somebody's wicked theories. I believe this language is deceitful and counterproductive, but profoundly revealing. The authors of it are hostile to children, parents, and arithmetic itself.

I do not believe that most children can do the things described in this paragraph. Can eight-year-olds "apply increasingly sophisticated strategies based on these properties to solve multiplication and division problems?" Can they divide at all? How many strategies are there?? What if kids simply learned to do one strategy really well? That's what teachers push if they actually want children to master arithmetic. But the one-best-way is the first idea killed off in many of these programs.

Throughout our lives, when we have math to do, we typically have to do it by ourselves. It is very handy to know the simplest approaches, to know them in a reflexive and automatic way. Everything in public schools takes you in the opposite direction. You know nothing automatically. You are trained to reach for a calculator but you don't even know if an answer is close. You are told to come up with your own way to solve every problem, and make sure you can explain your answers. So if you're trying to figure out how much paint to buy for a six-room house, you had better set aside an afternoon for this project.

The essence of successful education is to start at the very beginning, learn about and master the simplest things, and then steadily advance from the easy to the more difficult, over many years. Reform Math says, no, let's not master anything, let's learn 5th grade concepts that first year, and 3rd grade concepts and some college concepts too. The smarter kids, the ones who will go on to major in math, may find all this quite congenial. But that is irrelevant. This isn't a gifted class. The ordinary kids will be destroyed. No math will be learned, which seems to be the goal of the ideologues in charge.

────

I've been wondering if the Education Establishment, should they become serious about their work, couldn't simply take the best features from Saxon, Singapore, Math-U-See, Math Mammoth, Horizons, Switched-On, Schoolhouse, Abeka, et al. I even asked some of the people behind these programs: couldn't you create something to save the public schools? Well, they were smart enough to say, look, our programs are for home use and the public schools present special problems. Still, I can't help thinking that these people can provide the answers way before the National Council of Teachers of Math can.

I've been wondering if Bill Gates, if he wanted to help the public schools in the simplest quickest way, couldn't organize a team of America's most gifted math teachers (middle school level) to find the best programs, cull the best features, and create something called American Math, and give it to the country. Imagine a press conference where Bill Gates announces, "This is our gift to the American people. Our experts say this is the best, the easiest, the fastest. Everyone should start using it today. Arithmetic leads to higher math, and both lead to science and technology. We need every American to be skilled in these areas. Let's get cracking."

Instead he wasted a billion dollars trying to force Common Core on the country.

———

The Legend of John Saxon, Math Warrior

Warning, this article contains superlatives and extreme statements. How should we teach the young? I believe everyone should be passionate about the answers. The country's fate depends on it.

Over the years I often heard the name John Saxon but knew for sure only that his books were popular among homeschoolers. I was under the impression that he wrote his books for them. Not true. He wrote his books for every kid stuck in a classroom.

I've just finished *John Saxon's Story: a genius of common sense in math education*, an excellent biography by Nakonia Hayes. It is a smart, judicious book with 340 pages. It is not a potboiler, not really a page-turner. But it tells the life story of a totally remarkable man. I think it's correct to say that John Saxon is the greatest American educator of the last hundred years. He is unique in our history. If you want to understand the wreck that is American public education, read this book. If you are a teacher or parent hoping to defeat the treachery in the school system, read this book.

John Saxon—almost by accident, in a second career following 27 distinguished years in the Air Force—became a millionaire as writer and publisher. His books and his methods were that good. Oh, how the Education Establishment hated him for this. If the playing field had been level, I assure you Saxon would have been a billionaire. He would be to education and publishing what Steve Jobs is to computers.

The field was not level. The Education Establishment used its vast strength to promote Reform Math (an inferior approach) and to discredit John Saxon. This battle raged in most states and many cities, sometimes school district by school district, school by school, grade by grade.

Given the chance, most people chose Saxon materials because they worked. Fundamentally, John Saxon did what clever teachers have usually done if they are sincere about teaching a body of knowledge. Start with the simplest facts; practice; add more facts; review; etc. *Make sure students experience success.* We see this paradigm in every good French class, typing class, cooking school, and music school.

Evidently, the people in charge of the public schools did not want to teach much math. Reform Math (an umbrella term for a dozen separate curricula) was a flop that prevented children from learning basic arithmetic and drove millions of students away from chemistry, physics, and calculus. Reform Math was not just fuzzy and dysfunctional but racist and sexist. The premise was that girls and minorities cannot learn math. So a dumb-math must be created. The second sophistry was that all children must be subjected to dumb-math!

Saxon desperately wanted kids to learn. Think of a wise old football coach, by turns gruff, theatrical, and tenderhearted. Saxon was a fighter. He was also a shrewd theoretician. He had taken a lot of math courses, struggling with much of it. When he became a teacher, he was obsessed with finding better ways to teach math and everything else. He embraced what worked.

***John Saxon's Story* contains hundreds of anecdotes and quotations that illuminate Saxon's life. Some will bring tears to your eyes. Here is my favorite, a fan letter from a high school teacher: "I think perhaps there can be no higher compliment to you than to tell you how much feeling my students have for you. After 17 years, I know it is remarkable if a student could tell me the color of**

his math book—to say nothing of knowing who authored it. The Saxon students trust you and work hard and do well for themselves, for me, and for Mr. Saxon."

As child and adult, John Saxon was hyper-energetic, charming, and hard to manage. He preached that life should be an adventure. He joined the Army Air Corps in 1943, and learned to fly bombers. Before he could be sent to Europe, he was accepted into West Point, where he earned a degree in engineering in 1949. He was married and had four children. He survived four plane crashes. He was a combat pilot in the Korean War. After that, he earned a degree in aeronautical engineering so he could be a test pilot for five years. He got a Masters degree in electrical engineering at the University of Oklahoma and taught at the U.S. Air Force Academy. In 1968 he was ordered to duty as a pilot in Vietnam. Forced to retire in 1970, he hated it. He got counseling, and the idea came up that he should become a part-time algebra teacher at a junior college in Oklahoma. He was stunned that his students knew so little math. That's where the saga really begins.

Saxon criticized the professional educators for adopting programs that were not tested or proven. He ran hundreds of attack ads in the professional journals. He challenged their books to one-on-one tests, offering to cover expenses. Saxon promised that his "books will win—by an order of magnitude." There were no takers. Here's why: Reform Math is a loser, a tar pit where bad ideas go to become fossils. **An up-and-coming professor admitted: "The way that we typically do things in education seems almost reverse-engineered to produce the least possible learning." All my research says the same thing.**

Reform Math and Whole Word (Sight-Word reading instruction) are nearly identical twins. Rarely discussed in the same article, both are counter-productive pedagogies that keep children from learning whatever is allegedly being taught. Reform Math virtually guarantees that children will not be good at math. Whole Word virtually guarantees that children will be poor readers. Think of these two as the twin helix that spirals devastatingly through all the classrooms of America. Each of these phonies is a paradigm that exposes the other. You find the worst way to teach a subject, and then promote it with the full weight of the Department of Education, the National Education Association, the National Science Foundation, and dozens of groups with fancy names, such as the National Council of Teachers of Mathematics (NCTM).

If you told me the NCTM is a Communist front, I would think, now everything makes sense. However, if you insist that NCTM is composed of patriotic Americans, I would have to insist in return that they must live in Cloud Cuckoo Land. About math education, they are right as often as a stopped clock. John Saxon is right the rest of the time.

John Saxon died in 1996. We need him more than ever.

————

Price's Easy Arithmetic for First Graders

INTRODUCTION

New Math, which arrived around 1962, was supposed to be a better way to teach math to young children. In fact, it was complex, cumbersome, and, I can't help thinking, criminal.

The American people revolted almost instantly against New Math. It was unworkable clutter created, please note, by a consortium of upper-echelon professors, evidently the last people on the planet you should hire for such a task.

I can't say enough that New Math was a preposterous affront to good sense, and in my opinion could have been devised only by subversives. Fortunately, New Math vanished so fast, it couldn't do much damage.

Fifteen years later, however, the Education Establishment was back with Reform Math, an umbrella term for a dozen separate curricula. Trouble is, all of them are intellectual descendants of New Math. All of them use one recurring gimmick: mix simple arithmetic with high-school or college-level concepts.

The marketing propaganda says the children will thereby mature quickly in their understanding of math. So you teach children to add 7 + 18 to get to 25, but you do it with the help of set theory, Boolean algebra, base 8, and anything else that might make matters murky. Result: kids can't get to 25.

One big problem is that Reform Math specifically crusades against mastery. But it makes so sense to teach B, never mind C and D, until kids have mastered A. All you create is confusion. The long-lasting problem is that most kids, having been blitzed and bollixed at the age of 6, 7 and 8, never recover. They can't add up a simple column of numbers in a restaurant.

Laurie H. Rogers exposes the problem in a blog post, noting that the Law of Primacy states that people tend to draw on the skills they learn first:

"Primacy, the state of being first, often creates a strong, almost unshakable, impression. For the instructor, this means that what he teaches must be correct the first time. For the student, it means that his learning must be correct. Unteaching is more difficult than teaching … The student's first experience should be positive and functional in preparation for what follows" (*Principles*, 1974; a government publication).

Obviously, teachers of mathematics must do it right the first time, in the most efficient and precise way possible.

So it is against this backdrop of totally unnecessary and destructive complexity that I started asking myself a question: how would a clever person teach arithmetic in the simplest, quickest way? I wanted to go as far toward simplicity as the so-called educators went in the direction of chaos and confusion.

An answer finally came to me: you could teach all of first-grade arithmetic with pennies, nickels, dimes, quarters, half dollars, and dollar bills.

You start with five pennies. A few weeks later you work up to ten pennies and two nickels. A few weeks later you add dimes. A few weeks later you introduce the first quarter... All the while the children are learning to add and subtract every possible combination effortlessly and confidently. Little by little, they learn how to write down these combinations. They move slowly and painlessly toward the end of the year when they would be able to pay $4.56 for a toy, receive a discount of $1.83, and know how much they ended up paying.

The point is, all my instincts tell me that we ought to keep it as simple as possible, with virtually no abstractions, no jargon, no advanced concepts, no word problems, no nonsense about associativity, place order, and all the other stuff they teach in Reform Math and Common Core. The goal is that the slower kids sail along with the faster kids.

If you want to add extra complexity, let the kids play bingo, card games, and dice games. All human beings love card game and dice games, and these are an easy way to teach probability. You can also teach how many days are in a week, how many seconds are in a minutes—the basic numbers we all have to know.

Now let's look ahead to the second grade. Think how easy it would be to teach fractions, and then decimals, because ten cents is $ 0.10 and is .10 of a dollar and is 10%. Just different ways of saying the same thing. Similarly, a quarter is 25 cents, and is .25 of a dollar, and 1/4 of a dollar, and a "quarter" of a dollar. I think most kids, by the end of second grade would be able to understand that $.50 is one-half of a dollar and it's also 50% of a dollar, given that rock solid foundation that they got in the first grade.

There's another beautiful thing about using the dollars and cents—cheap. The Reform Math curricula probably cost 50 bucks a pop. They're elaborate, expensive, and destructive.

The point of my curriculum is to do elemental things easily, not to roam all over the countryside, learning to do 50 complex things poorly. The bigger point of my curriculum is to show the absurdity of using college-level concepts when all you want to accomplish is that children grow up to be comfortable with numbers.

I hope everyone appreciates that this article is more in the nature of a thought-experiment. What would simplicity look like? The so-called experts have carpet-bombed the educational landscape with spurious complexity. I feel there is something quite malevolent about this.

You can find on the web the Standards that each state has. Some of this prose is, as my father used to say, like death warmed over. Ever since New Math 60 years ago, the entire field is corrupted. I don't assume you will adopt my "Easy Arithmetic." The goal is to encourage you to design your own. Prune away the worst of the weeds. It's a start.

What about football fields??? I had an epiphany. Almost every school has a football field, all nicely laid out and divided into 100 units, with markers at the 5-yard line, the 10-yard line, and the 50-yard line. Think of all the arithmetic you can teach with this field—counting, fractions, and percentages. The dollar bill, the football field—a small and large version of the same thing. Surely these are the two best teaching aids possible. You could put kids in the bleachers; and then have other kids move around on the field to show various operations. The kids can see what 10% is, what two-tenths is, and the rest of it. Can't get to a football field? So find the biggest photograph or best online photo you can. Point is, kids are watching games every weekend. They see the chains moved up and down. They hear about third-down-and-five. The football field is such an obvious and wonderful teaching aid… why do I have the gloomy suspicion that no public school in America uses this technique???

————

You Might Almost Think Math Instruction Is Designed Not to Work

For a few years I thought the worst possible gimmick in education was Whole Word, basically a device to make sure kids don't learn to read.

In the last few months, the clamor grew about Core Standards and National Standards, and I started to focus on arithmetic. More and more I'm struck by the parallel with Whole Word. The Education Establishment seems to specialize in coming up with techniques that are almost guaranteed not to work.

I know there are sophisticates who will say, well, of course, everyone knows all that. No, many are blissfully unaware. In any case, the thing that fascinates me is the amount of skill and intelligence needed to create something that is not what it appears to be. Personally, I'm still stunned. Did people really go into a room and say: how do we teach math so that nobody learns math??? Well, it seems that way.

I think we can see the phenomenon best in New Math. Experts said it was the perfect way to teach math; but it was trashed only a few years later. The flaw was that easy arithmetic was mixed in with advanced concepts so that kids were too confused to learn even the basic stuff. Unfortunately, that central flaw was rolled forward into all the subsequent programs, for example, the many programs within Reform Math and now Common Core.

As so often happens in education, the public has to deal with this weird choice: are the people in charge hopelessly stupid or hopelessly subversive? For a sense of how bad things are, here is a scary report from math teacher C. F. Navarro, PhD (on the excellent site Illinoisloop. org):

"At the George Washington Middle school where I taught

eight-grade math in 1998, only a few of my math students were at grade level. The rest were at a fourth-grade level, or lower. Most had not yet learned their multiplication tables and were still counting with their fingers. By the end of the year some had progressed to about a fifth-grade level, a substantial improvement, but far short of the comprehension and skills required for algebra. Nonetheless, all were required to register for algebra the following year.

"More troublesome still was my algebra class. The students in that class were all nice kids, mainly from middle-class families and, therefore, on the school's 'talented and gifted,' program. Yet, with few exceptions, they didn't know how to work with fractions, decimals or integers. They lacked the power of concentration to set up and solve multiple-step problems. They were incapable of manipulating symbols and reasoning in abstract terms. Like most of my general math students, some had not yet learned their multiplication tables and were still counting with their fingers."

Could things really be that bad if the Education Establishment were sincerely trying to teach math? Isn't that hard to imagine?

So what is the answer? Many businesses and parents (with kids in public schools) have to consider tutoring (e.g., Saxon Math, Singapore Math, Math Mammoth, MathUSee). Next, the more I look at the National Standards and Core Standards, the more I hope that states will reject these federal proposals. If you're curious, go to corestandards. org to read some of these bizarre so-called Math Standards.

One of the distinguishing traits in the newer Standards is a gimmick called spiraling with mastery expressly outlawed. Children are moved quickly from topic to topic. Teachers introduce as much variety as possible. According to lots of testimony, it's confusing!?!

Nothing for me illustrates the absurdity of New Math, Reform Math and National Standards Math better than the insistence on teaching base-8, base-7, and other such nonsense to little children. What adult needs to deal with such irrelevant, esoteric knowledge? Not one in a hundred. But for a child it's even worse than useless. In base-8, the symbols 11 and 12, for example, have completely different meanings. A schizophrenia is introduced, a mental tension. I'm satisfied that nobody sincerely trying to teach arithmetic would mention such gimmicks.

The key word is "sincerely."

————

Reform Math Must Be Destroyed Root and Branch

The Education Establishment went way too far, and this has presented the country with a unique opportunity for real improvement of the public schools.

As never before, parents across the United States will tell you emphatically that they hate Common Core, and they especially hate Common Core Math.

The Education Establishment will try to maneuver around this revulsion. Compromises will be offered. The same dumb ideas will be repackaged as something new and wonderful. The challenge is to refuse to compromise. Sometimes a good thing, compromise is now the biggest threat to genuine reform.

Our Education Establishment has been selling inferior goods for more than half a century. They know how to bait and switch, and lie. Ordinary citizens stand little chance against these cunning maneuvers. So let's keep it strategically simple. Go for total victory. Reform Math should be discarded, inane root and goofy branch.

By way of background, Reform Math is a dozen separate but similar math curricula created in the 1980s. The most hated of these is *Everyday Math* (*Mathland* used to be the most hated but it has been buried, which is what we need in every case.) Here are some of the other titles: *College Preparatory Math, Connected Math, Core-Plus Mathematics, Discovering Math, Number Power, Interactive Mathematics, Investigations Math, Trailblazers, Chicago Math.*

But why did the experts create so many basically interchangeable programs? The answer is that when a community learned to hate one of them, the experts could say: *okay, you win, let's try this one...* **And they bounced the people SIDEWAYS from one bad program to the next. If you like cynical, you have to love this.**

During the 1960s, the Education Establishment watched New Math, in development for a long time, crash and burn in a few years. Parents laughed it out of town; schools went back to real arithmetic. Apparently, the Education Establishment did not want that same scenario repeated. So they cloned a dozen math programs. In that way, parents never really had a chance during the last 30 years. If they didn't like Tweedledum, they got Tweedledee.

Now the Education Establishment is cycling all of these crummy Reform programs forward under the banner of Common Core, thus the phrase Common Core Math.

The common denominator of all these inferior programs is an artificial complexity, and an emphasis on learning concepts and "meaning" without actually being able to do problems. These programs teach algorithms that parents don't know. A tremendous separation is created between the generations. Parents are rendered irrelevant. The children are frustrated to tears. In a few years, in all of these Reform curricula, the kids end up dependent on calculators.

The short-term effect is that fewer kids become skilled at math, The long-range effect is that millions of students are discouraged from studying algebra, calculus, physics, chemistry, etc.

So there is a sick joke here. The Education Establishment promises to help children understand the meaning. At the end the children don't know meaning, method, or anything else. Even if there is such a thing as the meaning of math, you would surely want to teach children how to count, add, and subtract first. Later, when the children feel comfortable with basic arithmetic, you could explain deeper aspects. The essential perversity of all Reform Math programs is to introduce the complex ahead of the simple. It's a bulletproof way to confuse little children, and our Education Establishment keeps exploiting it.

Clearly, the all-pervasive problem is that we can't trust our so-called experts. They are ideologues first, educators second, and therein lies the tragedy. These pretenders design curricula to achieve ideological goals. What we need from now on are curricula that achieve educational goals.

Almost no homeschoolers or private schools use Reform Math curricula. These programs are used when ideologues can gang up and bully the public.

The favorite programs outside of Reform Math are *Singapore Math* and *Saxon Math*. Both teach children how to do arithmetic in a systematic, logical way with mastery throughout.

John Saxon was particularly proud that students using his textbooks moved on, in far greater percentages, to algebra, calculus, etc.

Looking back at the sweep of American secondary education, the big event was the introduction in 1931 of an unworkable reading method known as Whole Word. The Education Establishment got away with it. Whole Word was in control in most communities until the end of the 20th century; and schools were turning out semi-literates by the million. We have to suspect that our elite educators saw this as the paradigm: a school pretends to teach something but makes sure that the children don't learn it. Whole Word does that. Reform Math and Common Core do that.

If you want to be really depressed about all this, keep in mind that the National Science Foundation pumped nearly $100 million (your tax money) into subsidizing hundreds and hundreds of professors as they drew up equally disastrous Reform curricula that would fundamentally undercut the study of science! Meanwhile, the National Council of Teachers of Math gushed approval of every little anti-math gimmick. All these front groups, pretending to be independent and impartial, keep pushing bad ideas on the public. The same pattern repeated itself with Common Core, which was supposedly given to us by the National Governors Association and the Council of Chief State School Officers (CCSSO).

So many credentialed experts; so many billions of dollars; so many secret intentions. The Education Establishment has everything but curricula that enable children to become good students. We may not be able to fire these faux-educators. But we can systematically eliminate the kind of poisons they like to inject. We can systematically take the attitude that the Education Establishment has proven itself incompetent, if not malicious, and from now on, whatever they're selling, we don't want it.

4. HISTORICALLY SPEAKING

One hundred years of dumbing down:
Our experts say they know what's good for us.

Education as Neurotoxin

More than a century ago, Maria Montessori reached a brilliant insight. Observing "special needs" children at an institution, she wondered: *Suppose we created a sensuous, mentally-jazzed environment that constantly challenged, provoked and inspired these young minds?*

Montessori acted on her insight. She created a new kind of school for supposedly retarded children. Very quickly, her students were equal to "normal" children. She became the toast of Europe; as she deserved to be. Montessori's vision has to inspire all true educators.

Unfortunately, American education, for a century, has followed exactly the opposite path from Montessori's. Our public schools are based on a model of intellectual minimalism.

The first question asked by John Dewey—and all agree that he is the Father of American Education—was this: how much content can we toss out the window? The second question was just as destructive: how can we teach school subjects so that all students remain more or less at the same stage? For Dewey the goal was never primarily an educational one, but a political and ideological one. He wanted cooperative children who work and play well together, who don't strive to get ahead, who are nearly interchangeable. Dewey hated the thought of an individualistic or superior child. He wanted to create cookie-cutter C-students who would welcome socialism. To do this, he and his followers devised what might be called the anti-Montessori classroom. The only positive stimulation was to come from group activities. Other than that, Dewey's classrooms, behind the contrived festiveness, were to be academically slow and stunted. The results would inevitably be numbing for many young minds.

None of this is subtle or arguable. If you confine children or animals to an intellectually bland environment, day after day, these creatures will hardly develop at all. Indeed, they will probably devolve. A lot of energy will be wasted on frustration, anger, resentment, and what might be called cognitive hunger. Children wouldn't have names for any of this. The children would merely shrivel inwardly and slowly wither. Education as neurotoxin.

Tragically, much of the genius of American Education has gone into devising dozens of methods that sound scientific or otherwise impressive; but in practice they don't work. That is, they don't work from the perspective of students and parents. They seem to work just fine from the perspective of the top educators at Teachers College. This perversity is so counterintuitive that you never stop being amazed by it. The facts, however, are clear. Consider the most egregious case of education gone bad. Whole Word was always sold to the public as "modern" whereas "dear old phonics" was dismissed as quaintly obsolete. Sounds good until we tally up the 50,000,000 functional illiterates and 1,000,000 dyslexics created by Whole Word. I would say that Whole Word is the purest example of education as neurotoxin.

Pause to consider the massive project required to create this bogus pedagogy, and then to enlist the parade of professors who would vouch for it, and finally to indoctrinate the hundreds of thousands of teachers who would be sent out to sell this non-starter to parents. Dewey's Gang was basically staging a slow-motion coup; it unfolds to this day.

Rudolf Flesch, in 1955, wrote something very haunting: "The word method is gradually destroying democracy in this country; it returns to the upper middle class the privileges that public education was supposed to distribute evenly among the people. The American Dream is, essentially, equal opportunity through free education for all. This dream is beginning to vanish in a country where the public schools are falling down on the job."

(Perhaps younger readers need to be reminded: Rudolf Flesch, the author of *Why Johnny Can't Read,* was the extraordinarily smart and decent man who led the fight against Whole Word. Read him. I'm sure you will find that any page by Flesch contains more sense than entire books by the pretenders he had to fight against.)

John Dewey and his people hoped, in effect, to reverse the American Revolution. Our stated national goal was to provide universal education, to give ordinary people the scholastic blessings that had once been enjoyed only by the aristocracy. All of this was unfolding on schedule in the late 1800s. And then came Dewey. In the name of his ideology, he was willing to dumb down an entire country, to propagate neurotoxins falsely labeled as education. Discarding all of his dishonest ideas should be our first order of business.

For Dewey and his ilk the operative phrase was "social engineering." I would argue that the operative words should be "intellectual engineering." **No matter whether kids are gifted or slow, they are best served by Montessori's insight that all children develop most quickly in a challenging, cognitively enriched environment. Dewey's disgraceful goal was to crush all children down to the same average size. Thanks for the neurotoxins, John. But enough already. What we need is education as neuro-enhancer.**

"The Educators Are Coming! The Educators Are Coming!"

Ever since history began, there were always bad guys trying to smash through the gates. Sometimes the barbarians had a bigger army or greater cunning; but by common agreement "barbarians" are always the less civilized, the less educated. They were the outsiders, rude and crude, trying to pull down temples of wisdom they did not value or understand.

Goths and Vandals, Visigoths and Huns, Mongols and Vikings—they showed up on your borders and you knew hell was upon you.

In the 20th century, the West viewed Communists as the new barbarians. A movie made in 1966—*The Russians Are Coming*—exactly captured the paranoia, the fear, the terror, that these Asiatic barbarians would swoop down on our society and destroy it.

Well, we've still got enemies outside the gate. But I worry that the most dangerous people we have to deal with today are already inside the gates. They live amongst us, eating in our restaurants, strolling along our sidewalks, occupying positions of power and responsibility, pretending to be more or less like us. Indeed, the crucial differences are hidden in the mental chemistry, the

ideological DNA. **These invaders resemble us, but they seem not to be human, not in the usual way. They are like the pod people in** *Invasion of the Body Snatchers*. **And like the pod people, they seem determined to convert humans into empty shells.**

How do they achieve this? With battle axes and catapults? No, nothing so brutally physical. With massed armies? No, nothing so overtly militaristic. Will they burn books? No, nothing so obvious.

Their weapons will be subtle and sinuous, like a good sophistry. They will make the content inside the books unreachable and unknowable. Much like the Director in *Brave New World*, they will remove oxygen from our brains until most people are a Delta or an Epsilon, menial workers who do not need to decipher words on a page.

Huxley predicted a cold technological future: "'And this,' said the Director, 'is the fertilizing room…After which they are sent down to the Embryo Store…We decant our babies as socialized human beings, as Alphas, or Epsilons, as future sewerage workers or…Future world controllers…Nothing like oxygen-shortage for keeping an embryo below par.' Again, he rubbed his hands."

Oxygen-shortage? Now that is subtle. You never know it happened. If you do, you don't care.

(With Controllers and Directors, we're talking about the people at the very top, the most powerful commissars, the elite educators. Not teachers, of course; they have little power. On an internet forum, I noticed people arguing about the propriety of the state superintendent receiving a salary of $300,000. A trivial administrative position, you might suppose; one that could be eliminated with scant loss to students or society. But perhaps you need to pay people $300,000 if their main duty is limiting oxygen.)

The "oxygen," in our case, is the ability to read, write, and do simple arithmetic, skills which are steadily diminished. "Oxygen" is knowledge and information, assets which must be kept rudimentary. "Oxygen" is tradition and character, intangibles which must be diluted and drained away until they are no longer recognizable. "Oxygen" is everything that, in 1900, was accepted as defining human-ness. That "everything" is the target of our new barbarians.

In 1983, *A Nation at Risk*, a prestigious government report, concluded that public schools seem to have been designed by an unfriendly foreign power. Note: Unfriendly. Foreign. Power. See, the barbarians had already arrived more than 30 years ago. They hid among us, pretending to be engaged in education but chiefly concerned with conquest, subduing us with social engineering and spirit-warping sophistries, producing ever more faux-education and anti-intellectualism, rendering the country dumb and dumber.

Their tactics were civilized and refined. And so silent. They know which is the superior race. They are. They know we are the barbarians in our own land. And thus they should inherit the earth, our earth. It's only fair.

Why else would we yield without a fight? Everyone knows the dirge of decline: 50 million functional illiterates, a million dyslexics, falling SAT scores, the "Jaywalking" people who seem to know nothing, falling national competitiveness, high-school graduates who can't read their diploma. Our brains must have been starved.

"The Russians are coming!" We get used to this phrase. We think that the barbarians are outside and will someday invade. No, our barbarians invaded long ago and live right here…

Or so you might suppose if you study the public schools.

———

So Many Excuses, or How We Know Elite Educators Hate Education

Judging by the record, our Education Establishment believes in teaching as little as possible. Indeed, the prevailing attitude seems to be one of pious horror. *Teach X, Y, or Z?? Heaven forbid!*

Presumably, these elite educators want students to know their own names. Once you reach that achievement, our Education Establishment seems bereft of any good reason why you, a student, might wish to know anything else.

My impression is that the education commissars don't want teachers to teach much, and they don't want students to learn much. The broader goal seems to be a world where people know next to nothing. This, of course, is a world easily manipulated and controlled.

My gloomy sense of the education landscape is that every hot new method, when you really examine its impact, actually functions to diminish knowledge in the classroom. I've studied Constructivism, Cooperative Learning, Self-Esteem, Reform Math, and several others,

58

and found them of dubious value.

In day-to-day operations, however, the Education Establishment does not need the fancy sophistries just named. Instead, educators rely on several dozen dismissive clichés that can be tossed without thought into any and all situations, should anyone dare to suggest teaching something.

Here, in no particular order, are the most common excuses for teaching little, very little, or nothing:

"Our children can't handle this material."

"Our children don't need to know that information."

"Our children learn this material at home."

"Children don't need to learn this. They can look it up."

"This material is too exotic and remote—we need to teach things that are relevant."

"This material is too local. We need to teach about other cultures."

"This material will offend girls. No sexism."

"This material will offend minority kids. We must avoid racism."

"This material is old-fashioned and no longer interesting to today's kids."

"This material is too trendy, We want substance."

"This material is too technical and should be taught at a later grade."

"This material is obvious and we don't need to waste time on it."

"Children today are not interested in things that happened long ago. History is not a good use of class time."

"George Washington is overrated; haven't you read Howard Zinn on this? Thomas Jefferson, too."

"This material assumes that people all learn in the same way. Our curriculum must cater to diverse learning styles."

"This material is too controversial, we can't possibly mention it in the classroom."

"This material is too boring; we don't want to put our children to sleep."

"This material is easy—kids learn it from each other."

"This material will create differences between the children; we can't have that."

"War is much too violent and might give children bad dreams. We should skip all the wars. Except the Vietnam War. There you can teach political truths."

"All that scientific and mathematics stuff. Who really needs it?"

"All the stuff about rich people, kings, and aristocrats—it's very inappropriate for our kids."

"Betsy Ross—that's so lame. The American Revolution didn't really have much place for women. Girls will be offended by the exclusionism. Skip the Revolution."

"Caring about the environment is one thing. But our kids don't need to know the names of insects, trees, and stuff."

"Novels? They are too complicated and far removed from the lives of our children."

"Adventure books? Our children don't need trashy stuff like that."

"Success stories? No, we don't want to give children unrealistic expectations."

"Technology and computers—kids learn that on their own. Look what they do with their phones."

"Poetry? Maybe a few by Langston Hughes."

See how easy it is!! Everything is either too simple or too difficult, too close or too far away, too blue or not blue enough. Soon, nothing is left. Classrooms are filled with a stunned and shimmering emptiness. You can stare a thousand miles in any direction and see nothing.

Remember Relevance? That was a big, overhyped fad in the 1970s. It dictated that everything taught in schools must be "relevant," that is, part of the child's life. Behind the scenes, "relevance" gave educators carte blanche for discarding most academic and scholarly material. Then came the 1980s, and the new fad was Multiculturalism, which dictated that children must study faraway countries, both in miles and years. Behind the scenes, this gimmick gave educators carte blanche for discarding most of the things that children should learn about their own country, culture, or traditions. See how beautifully all these gimmicks work together to grind into dust everything that, mere decades before, was considered essential.

The only good thing about all these excuses is that they do provide a litmus test. So-called educators who say these things are clearly more interested in deleting knowledge than in teaching knowledge. You know them for the non-educators they are. (Of course, you can now understand why these people hate testing so much. Tests would indicate how little the children know, and *that* must be kept a secret.)

What we need is an Education Establishment that loves

knowledge and wants children to acquire it. Start early and teach, teach, teach, because facts are both fun and useful. Schools based on any other principles are babysitting services or indoctrination centers. Or, as with too many public schools, both.

————

Why Do They Dumb Down the Schools?

Asked why he robbed banks, Willie Sutton famously replied: "Because that's where the money is!"

Similarly, if asked why they dumb down the schools, our top education officials would have to reply, if they are honest: "Because that's where the kids are!"

A century ago, John Dewey introduced a counterintuitive idea, that schools are not for schooling—that is, teaching, learning, thinking, all that academic stuff.

Forget about it, John Dewey said. Schools are for socializing children.

An interesting sleight-of-hand occurs here. Picture in your mind a large building with one, two or three floors, a big parking lot, lawns, and playing fields. Perhaps a gymnasium and a science lab...Ah, you think, a school!

Well, yes and no.

Everything physical about this place is consistent with what we used to call a school. The visible attributes are there. But everything that goes on inside the school, the emotional, mental, and spiritual attributes, let us call them, are completely altered.

Imagine a friend of yours was possessed by an evil spirit. From all appearances you're talking to your friend. But something is wrong. The malevolent look in the eyes is not what you remember; the voice is off. It's your friend, in other words, but it's not your friend. In fact, this apparition may be your enemy, plotting how to kill you. But your brain keeps telling you: this looks just like my friend. Shouldn't I try to be friendly?

Appropriately, you feel a lot of confusion, schizophrenia, cognitive dissonance, and fear.

These are the feelings that many Americans have about their public schools. These places seem to have been possessed by a hostile spirit. Even though the schools look much the same as that used to, they are not operated according to the same spirit and goals.

The typical American screams silently: But I liked the schools the way they were. What happened to those schools? What is this new thing just down the street from my house? I see some malevolence in the eyes. Something is wrong.

But nothing whatsoever is wrong if you trust the opinions of the education officials. Following John Dewey's prescription to a fault, they have converted the interior intellectual machinery of the school so that it serves a different goal and strives for a different victory. They put all the emphasis on the social life of the child. Unfortunately, they're not talking about singing around the campfire and learning to enjoy team sports. They're talking very specifically about an early childhood education whose chief function is to prepare children for a collectivized society. Everything is focused on how children work and play together. If they are functioning as a happy, enthusiastic GROUP—and we should keep repeating that word because that's what Dewey was mainly interested in—then you have a good school.

All else is secondary. The intellectual part is secondary.

The essence of the con was to make everything appear to be the same, even as heart and soul were ripped out and replaced. So we still have teachers, desks, textbooks, book bags, homework, and blackboards. You'd almost swear it's a school. But it's not. It's an odd sort of kindergarten from K to 12.

What a breathtaking concept. You treat little children as if they are little children. When they get older, you treat them as if they are little children. And when they're about to graduate from high school, you still treat them as if they are little children—unable to grasp difficult subjects, unable to memorize anything, unable to know the history of their country, unable to do arithmetic, unable to read beyond a primitive level.

It's always important to remember, I think, that voters never voted for this. Legislators passed no new laws. There were no editorials in the press, no speeches given at City Hall, no plank in a political campaign. So perhaps you're asking, how did all this change come about? Because John Dewey and another hundred people like him agreed that a transformation was required. They operated covertly; they were a cult, and I think the commonsense word is a conspiracy. They thought that socialism was inevitable. It was just a question of preparing for this new dawn.

John Dewey and his cohorts were steady and opportunistic. They knew socialism was coming, in just the way that similar cults believe in cap and trade, global warming, the new world order, or whatever. The big-league social planners decided we needed a new set of plans.

That's Dewey's great sin. He didn't care about individual students. He didn't care about the society that most Americans loved and wanted to preserve. He was a wrecking ball for a different sort of society. He cared very deeply about that.

Solution: first, know how the other side thinks; second, ignore their disingenuous theories and methods; third, return to an education that is cognitive, intellectual, and knowledge-based.

Stop using the school as an indoctrination center, that's really the solution.

Educational Decline: Inside John Dewey's Misguided Mind

What wrecked American education in the 20th century? We hear so many excuses, so much outright lying, it's hard to stay focused on the essential history.

In so far as you can blame one person for a large historical shift, John Dewey (1859-1952) is the guy who mugged public education and left it bleeding in a ditch.

You know John Dewey. The guy with the 200 IQ, the guy who wrote the equivalent of 50 books, the guy who seemed to live forever and remain a vital force in education for more than 60 years, the guy who had something to say on every question, you know that guy. He's a lot to deal with. Let me cut to the chase, and deal with just two doctrines (or compulsions) that dominated Dewey's thinking and devastated American education. Just two. And you will quickly see that when these two compulsions are allowed to take control of public education, you won't have what used to be called education.

First of all, John Dewey was a socialist, a collectivist, a

communist, use any word you prefer. He wanted everybody to be the same. He wanted to kill off American individualism. He wanted all the children in the room to be good little coworkers, cooperative, more or less identical.

Now, shine the spotlight on just this point: if you know something that I don't know, you move to a higher level, even as I move to a lower level. I'm a C or D student, while you become an A student, and thus my superior. Social divisions are opening up in a classroom which is supposed to exhibit undifferentiated equality.

What to do? It's obvious. *You must be kept from learning more than I do.*

John Dewey was relentless in downplaying the importance of knowledge, facts, everything that he dismissed in the memorable phrase "mere learning." But it's not the learning per se that he hated. It's the differences that learning creates. Ever since the beginning of time you had A students, B students, C students. The same spectrum of differences would be there in sports, music, salesmanship, leadership, military skills, yodeling, or anything else you could possibly do in any sphere of real life. School, by definition, was supposed to deal with the academic part of life. Naturally you would have good students and not-so-good students. But Dewey stood in the doorway and said: no! We are not having any academic stuff going on here if that leads to differences. From that point on, American education was make-believe and patty cake.

Put yourself in Dewey's mind. The vision he always pursued was the happy group of laborers—you see them in propaganda films—going off to work with a shovel over one shoulder and grins on their faces. *Heigh ho, heigh ho, it's off to work we go.* Dewey wanted to build a brave new socialist world right inside each and every classroom.

In sum, Dewey hated social distinctions. To prevent what he hated, he was willing to destroy everything that schools have traditionally done. Remember, Dewey lived until 1952 and he and his clones trained all the Ph.D.'s that controlled education in the 1970s, and those people trained the ones we have to deal with now. Their socialist manias are the reason we have mediocre public schools.

Second and quite separate, Dewey and indeed all of Progressive Education was obsessed with making school pleasant and unchallenging, of letting children blossom to their full potential through activity and play. The idea of forcing children to finish a task, of imposing demands, of expecting discipline and industriousness, all of this was said to be tragically oppressive for the child's tender spirit.

Siegfried Engelmann said a wonderful thing: "Our educators are fundamentally looking for magic." I've thought about this quote a lot in the last few years. What Engelmann is saying is that our educators actually believed they could throw puppy dog tails into a pot, say the right hocus-pocus, and children would magically know whatever it was you might want them to know. And all of this would be effortless.

Obviously, this approach is nutty and dangerous. You and I, as adults, know that if we want to learn to ski or play golf, to speak Chinese, to be a chef, to drive an 18-wheeler or fly a plane, we will have to go to school. Even though we are grown-ups, well organized, and sophisticated in many ways, we will still have to study, read our instruction books, memorize stuff, and take tests, and prove over and over that we are actually mastering the things we're trying to learn. The process might take months or years. We as adults know that we have a lot of work ahead of us. There's no other way.

But all of our public schools are built on the absurd notion that, given a bunch of ignorant, unsophisticated kids, you can wave a wand and achieve academic magic. Little teaching need take place, because children will miraculously absorb. Sure, just as you and I, no-talent beginners, can snap our fingers and shoot 72 in the next pro-am golf tournament. Magically.

What happens in practice is that the children are given The Worst Possible Preparation for gaining success throughout the rest of their lives. They are told they don't have to work to get an A. They are told that everything will always be easy and there is no need to hit the books and really study.

So much in public school education is essentially preposterous. This love of magic is destroying children because they go to high school, then to college, then a first job, expecting they can do little or nothing but still be successful. It would be far better for the children, and the society, to give them realistic challenges, to let them fail sometimes, and then urge them to try harder. Basically, life has only one perennial message: the greater our effort, the greater our chances. The public schools bury that message and for this we should hold our Education Establishment in contempt.

So, what's it like inside Dewey's misguided mind? It's a land

without facts, a world without work. In short, a realm almost insanely disconnected from real life.

Finally, if the permissive hippie parents next door want to raise their kids unkempt and undisciplined, maybe that's their right. But when those parents insist on raising YOUR kids the same way, you immediately see Dewey's essential sin. He wanted to use the power of government to bully others. Dewey looked at how America was raising its children and declared: not good enough. You must do it my way.

———

Education: Everyone Should Be Paranoid

I remember, when I was in college, hearing other students discuss "The Paranoid Style in American Politics," a famous speech (1963) and essay (1964) by Richard Hofstadter.

I was not interested in politics then and paid little attention; but I can testify to the respect these smart students gave Hofstadter's thoughts. I assumed they had substance.

This essay, over the years, became a drumbeat in the culture wars. The message was steady and smug: only dumb hayseeds from the South, and American primitives from whatever region, could possibly be so stupid as to be fearful—that is, paranoid—about that harmless mirage known as the Red Menace, that is, the Communists. Enlightened people knew there was no threat. This drumbeat became still louder as the Tea Party took shape a few years ago. When liberals in Manhattan wanted to dismiss the whole pathetic spectacle, they knowingly alluded to "the paranoid style." Alas, those poor benighted savages.

So I've been reminded a lot of Hofstadter's analysis, and prompted to look at it with more care. Conclusion: there is no there there.

Few things better illustrate the left-wing twisting of American academic and intellectual life than this little piece of fluff. It appeared a few years after Khrushchev was in the UN bellowing at the USA, "We will bury you." The Communists made abundantly clear their hope for world domination, even as the Kremlin was busy killing millions of its own citizens in the gulag. The sensible reaction for every awake American was to be frightened—precisely the reaction that Hofstadter claimed was "paranoid." (Which part of "bury" didn't he understand?)

Hofstadter shows us sophistry at its awful apex, where reality is rearranged so that normal seems abnormal, and vice-versa.

Recall that a version of this gimmick had been in play for decades. Workers, supposedly the beneficiaries of Communism, were often its bitterest enemies. What an embarrassment. Deep thinkers in the Kremlin came up with the theory of "false consciousness," which basically says any time a person disagrees with what the Communists want, that person is suffering from a "false consciousness." In simple terms, that person is crazy. This was in fact a routine practice throughout Communist society: people who disagreed with Party dogma were locked in mental hospitals.

What Hofstadter brought to American intellectual life, to use that term loosely, was the same spin. If you respond in a normal or prudent way to Communist threats, you are paranoid. So we see that Hofstadter wasn't even very original. He took an off-the-shelf idea used by Communists to discredit their opposition, and watered it down by the simple device of substituting the word "paranoid" for the word "insane." The Communists in Russia call their enemies insane. The far-left in the United States call their enemies paranoid. Same trick. (Let's note that Psychiatry was shamelessly ready to assist totalitarians in search of a pretext.)

The word "style" is the important novelty in Hofstadter's sophistry. Style is something you personally select. It's optional, it's superficial, it's like a new wool suit. If the suit doesn't fit right, if it itches, if it makes you look foolish, that is entirely your fault. You CHOSE the suit. If you had any brains, the sophistry suggests, you would not choose this particular style.

Hofstadter summed up his insight this way: "The paranoid spokesman sees the fate of conspiracy in apocalyptic terms—he traffics in the birth and death of whole worlds, whole political orders, whole systems of human values. He is always manning the barricades of civilization." Yes, Richard, and who started this verbal extremism?

Karl Marx announced that the first order of business was to abolish all private property. The second order of business was to abolish all religion (and force everyone to worship in the Temple of Communism). The third order of business was to abolish most of the things that most people valued about Western civilization. Stalin and his successors were salivating at the hope of overrunning Europe, and eventually crushing

America. That was surely the end of civilization, unless people did man the barricades.

The Communists brought a new Dark Ages to Russia. They wanted to bring the same blessings to the entire planet. But the instant you showed the least bit of concern, fear, worry, or hostility, Hofstadter declared you paranoid. And paranoid was bad, very bad.

Now this sophistry seems to me silly, like the visual one when you pretend to snatch a child's nose, and the child believes you did! Similarly, all the smart people stood around admiring Hofstadter's fine clothes.

After all, what is the braino professor doing here but name-calling? So's your old man! How deep is that?

Richard Hofstadter was a member of the Young Communist League and later progressed to Communist Party membership. He was in a tiny cult but wanted to pretend the other 99.99% of the population is sick. It's natural Hofstadter would write propaganda for his side. What's not natural is that thousands of professors would use his propaganda in the classroom to persuade millions of students that anyone not a liberal was less than human. In sum, Hofstadter came up with a wee bit of logical linguini and it was treated with reverence from colleges in California to universities in Boston, and by all the high-level institutions and publications in between. That supercilious reverence is the problem.

I write a lot about education now; and the bottom line for me is that the decay in the public schools is possible only because so-called "progressives" adroitly manipulate our intellectual life. I've argued that American public education is a swamp of sophistry. Everything is sort of a trick that promises one thing and ends up delivering another.

Embrace New Math and nobody can count. Adopt Whole Word and kids can't read. Let Constructivism into the school and kids learn little. Similarly, accept Hofstadter's thinking and you'll feel no alarm as clever subversives undermine your culture. Well, praise where it's due, our Education Establishment does one thing really well, sophistry.

The only way we can improve public schools is to identify the sophistries one by one and eliminate them. One good place to start is with Hofstadter's claim that fearing your enemies is irrational. On the contrary. As far as I can tell, the biggest enemies of public education are the people in charge of it. Until they do a better job,

we should fear them.

———

Education: Land of The Giant Bimbos

I've been reading lots of books about education. The writers often describe juicy conversations and revealing scenes, as quick ways to illustrate what has happened to public education. I've encountered many great stories about bewildered parents, befuddled kids, obtuse officials, and dazed teachers.

So from all this glut of gobbledygook (working title: *Slow Times at Ridgemont High*), what would be the most memorable?

In his 1999 book *The Conspiracy of Ignorance*, author Milton Gross tells about the day that Professor E. D. Hirsch appeared at a California school to explain the virtues of cultural literacy (Hirsch had written a book on the topic). He spoke to a meeting of principals and superintendents who asked what facts a first-grader should learn. Hirsch suggested that children should learn the names of the Atlantic and Pacific oceans and the seven continents.

One of the so-called educators wondered why children would need to know any of that? of what value was learning such information?

No one at the meeting, according to Hirsch, was willing to defend the idea that children might need to know such facts, or might actually enjoy learning them.

The assembled experts wanted an answer to this question: Would knowing such information make you a better person?

Hirsch's facts are the very starting points for Geography and History, for Science and Environmental Studies, for Weather and News. You have to ask yourself, if basic information like this is prohibited, what is left?

Are children allowed to know the name of the state they live in? How about the city? Are they allowed to know their own names?

Let's make a list of what such non-educators would want a first-grader to know. Clearly, it would be a tiny list, one that might fit on a name tag. But the child is going to be in school 20 to 30 hours each week. What will they be studying and learning all that time? Nothing, it seems.

Think about this scene often enough, and you may have nightmares. You are staring into the cruel dark heart of public education. It is run by people who are deeply contemptuous of knowledge and probably themselves deeply ignorant. Do *they* even know the names of the continents? Anyway, these principals and administrators clearly don't want your kids to know. Everyone must remain ignorant.

School will be an endless baby-sitting service, at the end of which the children will know little more than when they entered the school the week, the month, or the year before. If you rule out something as basic as the Atlantic and Pacific, you rule out 99% of everything.

I submit that the people in that meeting were cultural bimbos. But in fairness to them, they are the victims of a system, specifically, the so-called schools of education they were ordered to attend. They went there for a few years and obtained a Master's or a Doctorate. And all that time, they were asked to learn almost nothing factual from the real world. They took courses about theories of psychology and sociology, about philosophies of education, about the so-called problems of education and techniques of education. But nothing so banal as the name of an ocean.

Were these future educators themselves ever encouraged to become educated people? One suspects otherwise.

When you imagine a graduate school of education, you are voyaging into the Land of the Giant Bimbos. That's where they create the principals and superintendents that Hirsch addressed. People who find it highly suspicious and unreasonable that kids might be taught the names of oceans. Or anything.

The dumbing down of American public schools was accomplished by one main technique: demonizing knowledge. Remove facts; ignorance is what you get. That's straightforward enough.

But you have to find the sort of people who are actually willing to do the dirty work of kicking knowledge out in the street. Conversely, getting rid of such people would be a big first step toward recovery.

Quite simply, when knowledge again becomes the focus and first concern of public schools, we will have a rebirth of educational success. Until then, don't expect much.

5. THEORIES AND METHODS IN THE CLASSROOM

**Every fad turns out to be another poison.
But they are sold to us as panaceas.**

The Busy Person's Checklist of Bad Education Ideas

O kay, you're a busy person. You have only a few minutes to think about education.

Fine! That's all we need to take a quick look at the 10 worst ideas in the public schools:

1) Math is chaotically taught (children don't master even simple arithmetic).

2) Flawed reading instruction is used (only one-third of children read "proficiently").

3) Basic facts and skills are not taught (foundational knowledge is ignored).

4) Guessing is encouraged in all subjects (this is especially devastating in reading as real readers don't guess, they read).

5) Constructivism is injected into every course (children must "reinvent the wheel").

6) Group learning is everywhere enforced (children don't learn to think independently).

7) Memorization is scorned (children are discouraged from actually retaining any information).

8) Self-esteem is relentlessly pushed in all situations (do a bad job, get a gold star).

9) Handwriting is not taught even though this skill helps with reading, writing, vocabulary, etc.

10) Standards are kept low (fuzziness praised, precision disdained, sloppiness tolerated, ignorance accepted).

Our Education Establishment appears more focused on social engineering than on intellectual engineering. The result is that they tend to favor inferior pedagogical methods. That's what I believe this list is: ten inferior pedagogical methods.

There's an easy solution: get rid of them. Do the opposite of what each bad idea suggests.

All of these gimmicks are working behind-the-scenes 24/7 to undermine whatever education is offered in any given school.

Put aside for the moment whether a school is rich or poor, the teachers good or bad, the students smart or not so smart. Put aside all the factors usually said to be important. A lot of these items tend to be used as alibis or excuses. Typically, however, these are surface phenomena.

Look deeper, inside the gunked-up engine. That's where you'll find the ten worst ideas in education doing their damage.

Conversely, we can terminate these bad idea and quickly have a good school. That's a school where students typically do the following: Master arithmetic. Read fluently. Learn lots of basic knowledge. Don't guess and don't invent knowledge. They work independently. They retain (i.e., memorize) information. They earn praise by doing good work. They learn handwriting. They try to set high standards of accuracy.

———

Four Reasons Why Education Officials Hate Geography

It's easy to point out that public schools don't teach much geography. Explaining why is more complex. Here are four reasons why our Education Establishment scorns geography:

1) THEY ARE ANTI-KNOWLEDGE: For more than a century, there was a prejudice among our top educators against foundational knowledge (that is, basic facts everyone should know). John Dewey in 1897 preached: "The true center of correlation on the school subjects is not science, not literature, nor history, nor geography, but the child's own social activity."

2) THEY ARE ANTI-HISTORY: Our so-called educators also scorned history. In 1929 two of the biggest (Thorndike and Gates) echoed Dewey when they decreed: "Subjects such as arithmetic, language and history include content that is intrinsically of little value."

Of little value? When people know history, they can make decisions and deductions about where they came from, how other societies handled similar problems, and how we should respond to challenges now.

But our elite educators wanted uninformed, dependent children who would fit better into the new Socialist world that Progressive Educators hoped was coming. These ideologues wrapped history inside a containment-device called Social Studies, suppressing as much of it as possible, and making the rest shallow.

Geography and history go hand in hand. Diminishing one hurts the other. You can't study history if you don't first learn the names of oceans, rivers, states, mountains, etc.

3) THEY ARE ANTI-READING: starting in 1931, American public schools taught reading with a bogus method variously called Look-say, Sight-Words, Whole Word, etc. This gimmick required that children memorize the English language one word-shape at a time. A long, slow process.

Look at Dolch lists for fourth grade and you find easy words like "bug," "good," and "house." What you don't find is a single proper name or place name. The pretext for the phony Dolch lists was that these were the most common words, and in learning these words, the child was advancing rapidly toward literacy. But when does a child learn to read words like Nevada, Texas, Chicago, Hawaii, or Kansas, not to mention Benjamin Franklin?

Geographical names, anywhere in a child's life, would provide a warning bell that this child did not actually know how to read. How could the schools silence that warning? Geography must die.

4) THEY ARE ANTI-PRECISION: The most striking thing about geography is its intellectual purity. A city is in a certain location, it has a particular name, and there are many specifics one can learn about that city.

In geography, there is no ambiguity, no vagueness, no fuzziness, no aspect where one could say, well, you should guess. In short, geography is everything that Progressive educators hate. Consider that the capital of France is Paris. There is no way Constructivism can construct this. No way Self-Esteem can pretend you know it when you don't. No way that Cooperative Education will make it easier for children to know this fact. No way to think "critically" about this fact. It's just a fact. It is.

(Properly, a student starts by learning many little nuggets of information. At some point, the student can discuss these facts, compare them, relate them, and prioritize them. That's what critical thinking is. This phrase is meaningless, however, unless the student first learns many little nuggets.)

THE GLORY OF GEOGRAPHY

Geography is a foundation not just for history but for the study of geology, anthropology, archaeology, world trade, finance, government, environmental science, military history, surveying, early mathematics, and much else. Any school that skimps on geography is a phony.

Francis Parker is a famous educator who died in 1902. I want to close with a quote from his book *How to Teach Geography* (1885). Probably you never heard a teacher rhapsodize about *anything* the way Parker can carry on about a topic that many claim is dull and dry:

"Geography explains and illuminates history...To know and love the whole world is to become subjectively an integral factor in all human life; the resulting emotion arouses the only true patriotism, the patriotism that makes the world and all its children one's own land and nation. Geography is one essential means of bringing the individual soul an appreciation of the universal and eternal."

We need more geography; more precision; more foundational knowledge; and more passion for learning. We need a lot less of the foolishness that undermines these four.

––––––

The Conspiracy Against Testing

Evidently, the Education Establishment hates testing. We hear the jeers and cat calls every day in the media. In fact, this hostility has been a continuous refrain for 75 years. Do you ever wonder why?

Simple. Ever since the time of John Dewey, the Education Establishment has been in love with one axiom. The real reason kids go to school is to engage in social activities, not traditional academic pursuits. John Dewey and the other big players were emphatic about this: "mere knowledge," as Dewey put it, was a waste of time.

Bottom line: our top educators hate facts and content. Naturally they hate tests intended to measure the learning of facts and content.

All right, at this point, the plot is just getting interesting. Imagine you are the Education Establishment; you're building these ideologically pure schools; and kids are indeed playing harmoniously together all day, learning little. Really, it's almost Heaven on Earth. Except for one little problem. Parents. These troublemakers are always asking questions: Is my boy learning to read? Can little Susie do arithmetic?

Now we see the crux of the dilemma. Schools are expected to produce a report card on each student's progress. In the traditional sense, however, these students aren't making much progress. These kids do not know, often literally, which comes first, D or P. (Whole Word, as you may remember, forbade teaching the alphabet!)

Now, you see irresistible forces hitting immovable objects. The annoying parents want grades on things that schools have scant interest in teaching, never mind grading. Not only that, the parents actually want A's and B's so they are sure their offspring are on schedule and headed for college!

So now we run headlong into the logistical puzzle: how does the Education Establishment fix life so every kid gets an A despite knowing little or nothing?

The answer, again, is simple and has two steps:

First, **they attack anything that the typical person would recognize as a test.** They try to discredit the very concept of testing, from a simple quiz to the SATs. These things must be ridiculed and rejected, for any conceivable reason.

For example, we've all seen the relentless (and absurd) attack on SATs. I can still remember, perhaps 30 years ago, when *TIME* (or some such) screeched that the SAT had actually asked the meaning of *yacht*. How could anyone expect inner-city kids to know a word like that?! The SATs were clearly racist and stupid. The next thing you know, these tests would expect farm boys to know what a *subway* is.

Another stunt is to attack a test on the grounds that it doesn't require so-called critical thinking or higher order thinking, as if that were really the point for middle school children who don't know who George Washington is.

Second, while using every available sophistry to attack the concept of testing, they jury-rig new kinds of tests that the public, battered by endless propaganda, is supposed to accept as substitutes.

We've heard a lot about alternative assessment, a fancy name for testing in some different way. For example, instead of putting a car through rigorous tests, we could have a nice old lady drive the car around the block and give her impressions. What a smooth ride! The car gets an A.

The new jargon is *authentic assessment.* Typically, this is neither authentic nor assessment. It could be a teacher saying, John, tell me about the Roman Empire. And John says, "It was very big, and long ago, and they built a lot of things out of stones." The teacher says, "You have the feeling of the Roman Empire." And John gets an A.

Typically, in authentic assessments, the word "authentic" actually means subjective. The teacher is allowed to look at the student's life, scrapbooks, interviews, projects, and come up with an impression.

As far as I can tell on a fast impression, left-wing groups usually love the idea of undercutting rigorous tests. Progressives seem to agree that testing is inherently racist and unfair. Social justice demands what some activists call "fair test" or "test scores optional."

These people constantly whine about "teaching to the test," "drill and kill," and all the other cliches which make it seem as though children spend their days in bondage. For example, they are sometimes asked to memorize what 6 x 8 is, or where Japan is. Can you imagine the pain?

To really enjoy the grim humor and menace in all of the preceding, let's reflect on what our Education Establishment would do to the driver's test. Who cares about the rules of the road? What matters is, do you hate carbon dioxide emissions?

Imagine that your doctor or dentist is tested via authentic assessment. All that detail about blood types and germs is silly. Are illegal aliens given affirmative action, that's the main thing? Airline pilots? The real question is whether the pilots try to create harmony among the different peoples on the planet? And chefs? What's the big deal about taste? Surely the question is what ethnic group inspired her cuisine? of course, lawyers, CPAs, engineers, bureaucrats generally will soon know next to nothing, and the society will collapse.

Here's our dilemma. If kids go to school without learning the freezing point of water, what 7 times 8 is, or who Napoleon, Thomas Jefferson, and Buddha are, our Education Establishment doesn't care. My sense is that they're indifferent or even hostile to the most basic background information.

It's the very same hostility we see in all discussions of testing. The elite educators hate testing because they don't want there to be anything worth testing. Or worth learning.

I have to keep repeating this because they will try to persuade you that they have something serious to say about testing. They don't. They have only one thing to say—they don't like it, and want it to go away.

Many public schools have become fact-free zones. The people there don't teach much. The kids aren't asked to learn much. But nobody is supposed to notice. The last thing the education bosses want in these places is a real test.

———

How Schools Hold Children Down

Behold the mighty Gulliver, in the prime of his life held down by a few dozen strands. This has always been an arresting image. It seems paradoxical that such little ropes could restrain this gigantic creature. But let's imagine that instead of rope tied to pegs, we use piano wire secured to metal beams. Then you realize that probably even a mighty athlete could be firmly secured with ten or twenty thin wires.

It's simply a matter of having the right restraints cleverly arranged. You have to make sure the wires press down on the right parts of the body.

Let's consider the typical child in the typical school. What would you have to do to make sure that, education-wise, the child is adequately restrained?

Do you wonder why anyone would want that? Some political philosophies demand that citizens be kept under control. Some ideologies insist that all runners run at the same speed, otherwise the race isn't fair. Some officials are ruthless control freaks. Some elitists want everyone else kept in their place. Some pundits say: blame dumbing-down on greedy corporations. It turns out that there are many forces working against genuine education, and here are some of their techniques.

Suppose you could keep a child from reading right away. Indeed, many of the early Progressive educators believed that reading shouldn't begin until fourth-grade, so they were very comfortable with reading retardation. G. Stanley Hall, the professor who mentored John Dewey, thought that illiteracy was a satisfactory outcome for ordinary children. Parents, of course, didn't buy this malarkey; they were always pushing for literacy. What could Progressive educators do? They had to come up with ineffective reading instruction so they could *appear* to be teaching children to read; but almost no one would learn to read at a high level. Ordinary kids would be forever semi-literate. That in a nutshell is the history of Whole Word, which has stupefied tens of millions. If a child cannot read in a comfortable, capable way, you can easily imagine how little progress will occur in Geography, History, Science, Literature, etc.

But that's just a start. How would you keep a child from doing arithmetic? Numbers are everywhere: clocks and calendars, road signs and speedometers, buying things and counting change. Probably most kids would learn a good deal of math if you simply left them alone.

Here is the genius of New Math (and the later variations called Reform Math and Common Core)—it never left children alone. Even as these pedagogical interventions refused to teach mundane useful math, they relentlessly forced children to wander helplessly in advanced math. This was quite a clever trick. Most of the parents didn't know much math; so they were cowed into silence by constant references to algebra, geometry, statistics, set theory, engineering, trigonometry, pre-calculus, base eight, place value, properties of operations, and lots of other jargon. Who could be against such wonders?

These programs (New Math, a dozen varieties of Reform Math, and Common Core) were brilliantly designed. Children went all the way through high school, arrived at college, and still couldn't multiply 7 x 6 without a calculator. **(One persistent problem was that some children have a knack for math. How could such naturals be slowed down? Simple. You make all of math instruction revolve around** verbose "word problems." Many of these kids haven't been taught to be good readers. of course they will struggle with wordy problems. Problem solved.)

All right, now at this point the children don't have both arms, so to speak, but they're still running loose, they're seeing, hearing, talking. Educationally speaking, they are much too active. If teachers merely discussed interesting facts, these children could still learn a lot. So that had to be stopped. The name of this technique is Constructivism (or the Discovery Method). In this vacuum-friendly pedagogy, teachers don't talk about interesting facts. They are forbidden to do so! Rather, the children are supposed to discover facts for themselves. As they can hardly read or count, they will discover facts only in a very rudimentary sense. Still, they are made to seem busy all day. This shuts up the parents.

No reading, arithmetic, or knowledge. You underestimate the commitment of our Education Establishment if you think they stopped here. No, they came up with many more devices for making sure that the education-elevator remains permanently on the first floor.

Self-Esteem, for example, dictates that children should not be allowed to feel badly about themselves. If some children learn more than others, the ignorant children will lose self-esteem. This evil cannot be permitted. The key is to make sure that everything is taught to everybody at the same low level.

Cooperative Learning, another leveling device, has been remarkably successful at eliminating some of the last vestiges of traditional education. Children work in groups of about six. All children are doing essentially the same thing; typically they are engaged in a project. Usually it will be something that sounds very grand, for example, Environmental Priorities in the Third World. The big feat here is that the children will use Google to find enough phrases to create a portfolio or poster listing those priorities. What each child actually understands might be very little; what they remember next year might be close to zero. But if all children have a high opinion of themselves, and parents think, look at this fancy stuff my kid is working on, that's enough. Meanwhile, children never learn what it means to be independent and self-reliant.

With the technique called **Learning Styles**, children are divided up according to a new sort of "racism": you have kinesthetic learners, auditory learners, visual learners, and many other kinds. Teachers expend a great deal of time and energy trying to figure out what kind of learner each student is, so they can tailor their lessons to fit various sorts of brains. Teachers are already exhausted before the first instance of teaching takes place. Learning Styles is something like karma and astrology combined. If you had a past life as a lion but your moon is in Taurus, no one can be surprised if you don't succeed. Learning Styles is an all-purpose alibi when schools do a bad job.

Another determinist technique is called **Prior Knowledge.** This one is particularly bizarre. The central premise is that children know lots of old stuff, and it will surely get in the way of learning new stuff. There is almost nothing anyone can do. The old stuff will sit there like an overturned truck in the middle of the road; traffic can't advance. The teacher must be very careful to catalog this old knowledge and struggle bravely to escape from its grip. But according to some theorists, Prior Knowledge is like having a genetic defect. You're stuck with it. (Note that the central trick in all of these techniques is to make sure the victim is at fault. The deep problem usually turns out to be something in the child's past or in the wiring of his brain. Certainly, schools cannot be held responsible if children show up with genetic defects.)

Still another cornucopia of bad outcomes is made possible by a relentless emphasis on **Guessing** and fuzziness. Close is good. The one correct answer is never glorified, indeed it is scorned. Children are told to indicate various ways of possibly trying to find an answer. These hapless children are expected to use context clues, picture clues, and prior knowledge. They should talk it over with their group, and take a shot. If they can show any reason at all why they came up with the answer they did, they can get an A.

Now just for fun, imagine that each of these children actually knew the right way to find the answer, and then found it. Think how satisfying that would be for them. But that sort of euphoria might encourage children to be more serious about their education, exactly the opposite of the desired goal.

So you see, it's just one wire after another stretched tightly and tautly across the bodies and minds of children. Each of them is a little Gulliver tied down by a swarm of lilliputian con artists.

———

The K-12 Lobotomy

An acquaintance sent this note: "My sister tells of teaching math to college freshmen. The question was: If X plus 5 = 10, what is the value of X? It took her an entire week to get the kids to finally say '5.' So the following Monday, just on a hunch, she gave them another problem: If Y plus 5 = 10, what is the value of Y? And no one could answer!"

Remember, these students have been admitted to a community college. Presumably, they studied Algebra around the ninth grade. The teacher is an experienced veteran who knows mathematics.

How can anyone explain this anecdote?

You would surely conclude that public schools did a terrible job. But the situation seems more ominous than even this summary suggests. These students have been made dumber at 19 than they probably were at 12. They can't understand a simple idea, even when it's explained to them for days. It's almost as if someone had performed a long, slow lobotomy on these young brains.

How do the public schools achieve this diminishment?

Suppose you were serious about achieving exactly that evil goal. Here are techniques you would automatically use. Whole books could be written on each technique, and probably have. But I'll be brief. It's the totality of the effect that we need to contemplate, not the details.

1) You ensure a general disorderliness, with lots of interruptions and chatter from loudspeakers. Discipline is slack. Ideally, unmanageable students are kept in the classroom. If children feel insecure and frightened, that's helpful.

2) You curtail or eliminate recess and physical activity. You want the children confined and lethargic, or bored and restless.

3) You divide students into small groups. They are graded as a group, praised as a group, and addressed as a growth. They learn not to trust their own thinking.

4) You keep children constantly engaged in trivial "activities." They sing a song or talk about their favorite day of the week. What matters is that the activities have no academic content.

5) You ensure that the classroom does not contain maps, especially of the US or the world. Geography is rarely taught.

6) You make sure that teachers think of themselves as facilitators.

They do not communicate information to the students. Teachers emphasize that facts need not be memorized. History and science are hardly taught.

7) Literacy is constantly referenced; and the classroom is filled with books. However, the methods used to teach reading are designed not to be effective. (The central sophistry is to teach English, a phonetic language, as if it's a hieroglyphic language.)

8) Math is referenced every day. However, the methods used to teach arithmetic are designed to be ineffective. New topics are introduced helter-skelter. Often these topics are exotic and complicated. Weird techniques are taught. Even in the sixth grade, most children can't multiply and divide, and don't understand decimals and fractions. They are dependent on calculators.

9) You insist that grammar and spelling are obsolete; cursive is a waste of time; kids shouldn't learn a second language. Anything rigorous and logical is dismissed as "inappropriate for our children." It's important to create an atmosphere where deadlines don't matter, tests are soft, grades are inflated, everyone is promoted, and students learn that little is expected of them.

10) The goal is that most students feel at once overwhelmed and empty. They know they are ignorant and barely literate. Whatever education is, they didn't get any. Many have been told they are dyslexic or have ADHD. Many have received tutoring, counseling, or sedation. Many pretend to be sick so they can stay home.

11) All educational failure is blamed on factors the school can't control. Children are said to be not ready, not smart, or neurotic in some way. Parents are said to be not involved, not helpful, or hostile to the educational process. The schools constantly praise their own wisdom and performance.

The totality of these eleven techniques, kept in play month after month, virtually guarantees that no education takes place. If some students are stubborn and insist on acquiring information on their own, they are labeled "gifted" and removed from the general population.

The whole process is carefully anti-educational and anti-intellectual. Whatever a real school would do, you do the opposite. A remarkable thing happens. The children grow physically; they age before your eyes. But what they know at 10 or even 15 is not distinguishable from what they knew at 7. What they know as high school graduates can be measured in smidges. They arrive in community college able to drink, drive, vote, serve in the military, or marry, but unable to grasp that if Z+5 equals 10, Z must be 5.

Much more than we would like to think, the K-12 experience is a lobotomy performed in slow motion.

McKinsey & Company, a famous consulting firm, put it this way in 2009: "The longer American children are in school, the worse they perform."

Postscript: Robin Eubanks, an attorney, has published a tough new analysis of the public schools, *Credentialed to Destroy*. She coined a phrase for what they do there: "mind arson." That's the same thing I'm talking about with the phrase "K-12 lobotomy."

———

Constructivism: Why It Hurts Minorities and the Poor

Summary: Constructivism is not just anti-knowledge, it's also anti-minorities and anti-poor. The less you know, the less you will *ever* know, thanks to this destructive gimmick.

Constructivism is the latest fad burning through American public schools. Here's a quick definition: children are supposed to invent their own new versions of all knowledge, while teachers (now called facilitators) are supposed to stand back and encourage the process.

I've been writing for some years about how unrealistic and time-consuming this approach is. There are thousands of things that a child should know. Children would need many extra years to reinvent the main facts of biology, history, arithmetic, geography, etc.

Even worse, children are supposed to build on what they already know (prior knowledge) and work at their own pace, So the class is automatically fragmented into many levels and points of interest. Let the chaos begin.

As noted, I was satisfied that this thing is not a good idea. But I've recently received a number of letters from teachers lamenting their classroom situations, and I now realize that Constructivism is even more of a menace than I supposed.

To put this in perspective, first consider older students, in college or even high school, with a good education up to this point. They know a lot of information and thus have a chance of reaching some new insights or generalizations. Now extrapolate downward to younger, less informed children. Their prior knowledge is very meager. *What is the child supposed to build on??*

Let's also extrapolate from the children who grow up in educated, talkative, involved families. Isn't it obvious that these children would know much more than the children from poor homes, deprived homes, homes where the parents are not well educated, and not very interested in the education of their children? **Such children know almost nothing. It's precisely these children most urgently in need of a crash course in foundational knowledge!**

What they get instead is an officially approved policy guaranteed to prolong their ignorance. Let me spell this out so there can be no misunderstanding: the younger and more ignorant the child, the greater the damage inflicted by Constructivism.

Now the following two letters from teachers will be self-explanatory:

"I was told today at a job interview that, even though I get great results with my students, they would rather hire someone who already believed in Constructivism....My kindergarten students can dissect a sentence like a second grader, and I am very proud of that. Still, I get marked down and ridiculed on my evaluations. My superiors complain that I need to have my students in cooperative groups (useless chatter), in learning stations (playing with toys), and that I need to refrain from correcting children for their mistakes and instead guide them with poignant questions to the right answer. I could spend a whole day or longer probing and cueing a child to give an answer, when he/she doesn't have the frame of previous knowledge from which to derive the answer." (Lynn M.)

"The principal has refused to recommend me for employment as a teacher because I flagrantly ignored the school's emphasis on education reform (read Constructivism) according to him. He was appalled that I had the students memorize facts. Where was the higher order thinking involved in the task, he queried me—not waiting for an answer and clearly not wanting one. It mattered not to him that the kids loved the geography unit. That they had learned about the equator, they had seen images of maps and had talked with me about how the world seemed to grow over time in ancient maps. We talked about technology and how our planet looked on Google Earth. We talked about the invention of the wheel, of navigation, and all sorts of other fascinating things. The boys were wondering if we would soon have Google Moon and Google Jupiter. They knew what a compass rose was and what it did. They learned about scale and computed some simple scale problems. No, none of that mattered because I had violated two major rules—I had had the children memorize facts and I had taught them information." (Jan H.)

For me, these letters are inexpressibly sad. These teachers are caring and conscientious but all that counts for nothing in schools that have declared war on facts. This war has been in progress for almost a century.

Constructivism is just the cleverest new tactic in this war. But unlike the previous tactics, which taught less to everybody across the board, this new tactic discriminates against the under-educated. The less you know coming in, the less you will be allowed to know, ever. Constructivism is just a highfalutin gimmick for dumbing down the next generation. Like so many methods called "progressive," it is actually regressive and repressive.

Schools must return to the knowledge business. This need has never been more urgent. Facts are fun. Knowledge is power. Start from these simple premises, and excellent schools are almost inevitable.

———

When Is Drill and Kill Not Drill and Kill??

If there is one true cancer in the land of education, according to our Education Establishment, it's the torture known as "drill and kill."

Progressive educators always hated Drill and Kill. It hurts the child, we are told, and is the end of genuine learning.

For the last hundred years, our Education Establishment condemned the direct transmission of knowledge from teacher to student. These elite educators are constantly in a rage that students might be forced to prepare for a test in the traditional sense, that is, they know facts.

And yet, when it helps their agenda, the commissars will betray their own pronouncements. Suddenly, 2 + 2 equals 5, or else. (George

Orwell, in his disquisitions on totalitarianism, explains that when power is the goal, Truth will often be tortured until it submits.)

Thus, evil Drill and Kill turns out to be the most wonderful perfect answer to your child's literacy needs. Thank you, Big Brother.

There is one essential skill, and it is reading. However, from 1931 to the present, our Education Establishment embraced a defective method called Whole Word. The essence of this method is memorizing words as designs or Sight-Words. Not a few words but all the words—that was the dogma for 70 years. (Now the modified dogma is that children must start by memorizing 220 high-frequency words, such as *see, it, is, was, run.*)

And how are these words to be memorized? There's only one way. You stare at them, draw them, and name them on flash cards, over and over, until your response is automatic. In short, Drill and Kill (a.k.a. "rote memorization") is the essential ingredient in learning to read, according to Whole Word theory.

So now Drill and Kill is a GOOD thing. In kindergarten and first-grade, and sometimes into second and third grade, kids are drilling and killing their little brains in an attempt to memorize the English language as graphic designs. It's difficult for smarter children, and impossible for average children.

So here we have a total about-face of the most blatant and dishonest kind. At this point, we might want to stop and marvel at the shamelessness of our Education Establishment. They are saying that 2 + 2 equals 3.

Here is a list of words that one might want to savor: obvious, transparent, evident, manifest, unambiguous, open and shut, clear, straightforward, unequivocal, unmistakable. All of these words describe the obvious duplicity and hoax of saying that Drill and Kill is lethal and then, when convenient, saying it's delightful and exactly what kids must do.

The amount of Drill and Kill required to memorize even 100 Sight-Words is huge. A program now used in some schools aims, in the first year, for only 36 words. If the expert is saying that 36 is a year's work, you know this is a very hard task indeed.

Meanwhile, the relatively modest amount of memorization required to learn American history, biology, etc. is quite doable. It's a good thing, even fun. Children learn a few facts each day and as the weeks and months go by, they become expert. But, as already noted, knowing facts is scorned, so our Education Establishment labels the whole business Drill and Kill, and tries to prejudice the community against it, thereby undercutting most academic progress.

It is unpleasant to contemplate the truth here. Drill and Kill, in the amount required to memorize the English language, is a hopeless project. One can only conclude that the Education Establishment never wanted children to be good readers, just as they didn't want them to know much factual information. **So they prescribed, at each point, exactly the medicine that would do the most harm.**

Orwell wrote about the ability, among the party elite, to accept contradictory facts. The party member has to show endless enthusiasm for whatever is said to be true. One week they love a country; the next week they hate the same country.

Unfortunately, our public school teachers are conditioned in the same way to hate Drill and Kill, and then to turn around and require Drill and Kill in the teaching of reading. Arguably, teachers are as much the victims of this perversity as students and parents.

But what about the professors at the top, the ruthless elite orchestrating all this turning on a kopeck? Surely they see the huge contradiction. Or are they such good party members that they actually don't realize that they are living in a dishonest, self-contradictory world?

————

"They Mean Well… Oh, Really?!?"

Perhaps the most repeated cliché in American education is this: "They mean well. They just can't get their act together."

Teachers, parents, politicians, and editorial writers repeat this cliche when they want to forgive the Education Establishment for creating so many destructive policies and dumbed-down schools.

It's a sweet and hopeful sentiment. Unfortunately, it's not true.

They don't mean well. And they have got their act together. That's precisely our problem.

A hundred years ago John Dewey and his followers settled on this formula: they would take over the schools of education; they would brainwash future teachers to care more about social engineering than traditional education; and those teachers would go forth into public schools everywhere to brainwash kids and their parents into being comfortable with less education. That, clearly, is having your act together. We see malice aforethought, and a steely dedication to a subversive agenda.

It's hard for most people to deal with these assertions. The ordinary parent does not want to believe evil about local schools; so there is a built-in disconnect, a willing suspension of distrust. It's much the same reluctance we would have about local priests, politicians and community leaders. We don't want to believe bad things about the people who run our lives. It's painful. Also, we may have helped put those people into positions of power; now we have to confront the fact that we didn't do our homework and we voted for dangerous extremists. That's exactly what happened.

If people want to save the schools, they have to become more cynical and astute. In practice that means acknowledging that our Education Establishment has had its act together for a long time.

All the bad policies adopted by our elite educators are premeditated acts. All their bad results are just what they were hoping for.

Hard to confront, isn't it?

When Charlotte Iserbyt titled her famous book *The Deliberate Dumbing Down of America,* she didn't mean "accidental" dumbing down, she meant "deliberate." That is, our Education Establishment was conspiring, plotting, scheming, planning, maneuvering, any word you want. These top-level educators are all socialists much like Obama and, no matter what they say to us, their real goal is always the "fundamental transformation" of the country.

When Robin Eubanks titled her book *Credentialed To Destroy,* she didn't mean "nurture and sustain." She meant *destroy.* That's the goal.

So when bad ideas get bad results, it's not appropriate to act surprised. The bad results are the whole point. The Education Establishment doesn't mean well at all; and they got their act together long ago so they could act on their socialist dreams.

The whole reason they came up with Look-say (a.k.a. Sight-Words) is to make sure children wouldn't learn to read or think at a high level. The reason they came up with New Math (anybody who takes a few minutes to study New Math can see this) was to make sure that most children would probably never master anything beyond basic arithmetic. The same goal was pursued more subtly in Reform Math.

The whole reason they came up with Constructivism was to take the emphasis away from teaching facts. Instead, they would pretend that kids would discover facts for themselves. This approach virtually guaranteed that at the end of each year there would be a net decline in the amount of information learned. That was the goal. That's the "deliberate dumbing down" that Iserbyt wrote about.

Our Education Establishment was secretive and sly, but they never thought small. First, they massively diluted the content part of education. Second, they sabotaged the instructional methods used so everything that kids learned would be garbled. Third, they undermined the character of the students, making them guess, letting them be late, telling them they were wonderful even if they didn't bother to study or do their homework.

There was almost no detail left out, so completely did these "experts" get their act together, so completely did they mean to start a war against their fellow citizens.

As Robin Eubanks argues in *Credentialed to Destroy*: "The point of Radical Ed Reform anywhere in the world has always been to use education to gain politically unpopular broader transformations and avoid detection until it is too late. By then the transformation would be complete at the level of the consciousness of the individual citizens... Or at least a voting majority of them. It is to be painless supposedly. No one need feel a thing. And if that scenario seems like a bad movie and you want to speed through or click the channels? We wish. This is precisely what happened and it is still going on."

Eubanks argues that Common Core is simply another reiteration of all the bad ideas the Education Establishment tried to perpetrate in previous decades.

———

How Ideology Is Killing Education (And So Much Else)

Background: Left-wing revolutionaries echo a theme: destroy everything, start over, who cares how much misery is caused if there's a better world in sight?

A teacher in Florida summed up the educational situation in her state: "There is an obsession with the worse-off students."

School officials there proclaim: "But what about the people with pathologies? They can't advance very far. It's fairer if we bring everybody along together."

Notice there is no obsession with curing the pathologies, or with devising better methods to help disadvantaged kids rise above their disadvantages. No, the answer is to reduce the better students to the level of the worse students. Where does this go?

Suppose that half of the people in your city are sick. Do we best help them by making the other half sick? Yes, according to leaders in our Education Establishment. To me this is an especially repellent sophistry.

When all are sick, who is going to solve the crisis and lead everybody back to health?

Schools cannot be in the business of trying to predict winners and losers. Nobody knows what will unfold 10 or 20 years from now. Why not give each child the best possible education that human ingenuity can devise? In this way, students are better off, no matter each one's destiny. Society is better off. Quite simply, the proper goal of public education is to push every student as far as each student can go.

Unfortunately, many in the Education Establishment have exactly the opposite goal. They follow the Progressive (that is, Socialist) teachings of John Dewey. They believe in leveling; they are working to achieve "equality of outcomes."

Elite educators speak a great deal these days about "fairness" and "social justice." When you hear these phrases, be very afraid that millions of students will be given a shabby education *on purpose*.

After all, what's the easiest way to achieve equal outcomes? You educate downward. You give everybody the same inferior education. But how can this be described as "fairness" or "justice"? Only far-left ideologues think this way.

So here we come to the essential immorality. In order to serve their philosophical beliefs, some in education's top echelon are willing to dumb down millions of children.

Pretending to care about the down-trodden but making sure everyone is down-trodden—is this ethically defensible?

The central problem is that the Marxist goal of redistributing wealth has been jury-rigged into education, where this ideology

morphs into a demand for equalizing knowledge, educational results and, if possible, intelligence.

Annie shouldn't have more than Debbie. Everyone must know the same things. Everyone must get an A. And there is the death of education.

It's not just the ideology per se that is undermining education. Maybe a little Marxism could be helpful. Here's is what is really killing us: the willingness of extremists to pursue their logic to the bitter end. When these social engineers talk about "bringing everybody along together," they mean one big herd.

What goes on in the minds of such fanatics? Can you stand to look into their dark hearts? Consider Cloward (now deceased) and Piven, two far-left professors who hatched a cruel plot for destroying the US economy as a way of advancing Socialism.

Here's how Jeannie DeAngelis summarized Cloward-Piven: "The duo taught that if you flooded the welfare rolls and bankrupted the cities and ultimately the nation, it would foster economic collapse, which would lead to political turmoil so severe that socialism would be accepted as a fix to an out-of-control set of circumstances. The idea was that if people were starving and the only way to eat was to accept government cheese, rather than starve, the masses would agree to what they would otherwise reject."

Aren't these professors some cold, cold fish? They want to serve humanity by making everyone destitute and desperate. And what will victory look like when all are crushed? Most probably the end of civilization as we know it.

The entire society or only the schools—it's all the same program. Overload the system, make it unworkable, until it runs off a cliff. Would such extremists shy away from dumbing down public schools, all the way to the lowest common denominator? of course not. If they could snap their fingers and make all children the same, they would do it.

Consider Bill Ayers, once one of President Obama's closest friends and confidants. Ayers said: "I get up every morning and think, today I'm going to make a difference. Today I'm going to end capitalism. Today I'm going to make a revolution."

This guy is now a professor of education. He used to fight capitalism by blowing up banks. Now he wants to blow up public education. Would he hesitate to remove any smidgen of intellect that remains in his way?

Finally, with heartless theoreticians like Cloward-Piven and Ayers in charge, the weight of educational failure will collapse the school system, just as the weight of economic failure will collapse the society. That's what we see all around us. That's what these fanatics work to achieve.

And what is the answer? Point out the obvious: there's no "fairness" in making everyone illiterate and ignorant, no "social justice" in mutual poverty. These faddish phrases are rhetorical frauds.

———

Bloom's Taxonomy: "What Do You Think About **X**?"

Sixty years ago, Benjamin Bloom came up with what he said was a superior way to categorize educational goals and activities.

The Taxonomy was famous for reducing everything to six steps: remembering; understanding; applying; analyzing; evaluating; creating. Note that "remembering" (or "knowing") is the LOWEST step.

Bloom concocted this taxonomy to describe education at the college level. College professors, however, ignored the Taxonomy. Meanwhile, the people in charge of our public schools put this thing on a pedestal. Why? Because the Taxonomy scorned what had always been considered the most important step, i.e., knowing information.

Bloom and his Taxonomy ended up being a favorite theory among Progressives who had, from the start, been anti-knowledge and anti-content. The top professors, as early as 1929, sneered at "subjects such as arithmetic, language and history."

The Education Establishment was hostile to knowledge, any and all knowledge. The question was, how did they make this hostility respectable? That's where Bloom's Taxonomy came in. Here was an allegedly scientific picture of what happened in a child's mind. The least important aspect was learning facts. The Taxonomy says so!

It's not clear whether Bloom knew his Taxonomy was a sophistry. Perhaps other professors perverted his noble intentions. The end result is the same. The symbolism of putting learning or knowledge at the *bottom* of the pyramid was clear to everybody. It was the trivial step. Why not just skip it?

(To restore sanity to Bloom's Taxonomy, put the word "facts" in each of the steps: memorize facts, understand facts, apply facts, analyze facts, evaluate facts, create facts. Then the message is fundamentally correct: start with facts and stay focused on facts.)

Our Education Establishment, however, went in the opposite direction, pretending that knowing was lower-order thinking, so children should jump ahead to HOTS—Higher Order Thinking Skills.

A fact-free world is like teaching a child to play tennis without net or tennis balls. You tell the child "Work on your forehand," but the child is not actually playing tennis. How can he improve?

In effect, Bloom's Taxonomy gives schools permission to be bad schools! Bloom's Taxonomy, by focusing on what is supposedly happening inside the child's head, suggests it's the child's responsibility to organize and master information in the most efficient way.

What nonsense. It's the responsibility of educators to organize information so that children can learn it quickly and easily. Instead, we have nihilistic hacks hiding behind Bloom's Taxonomy.

Bloom's Taxonomy is a misdirection, much like magicians and con artists have always done. The burden is on little children to be efficient, so adults can be sloppy.

Thanks to Bloom's Taxonomy, knowledge is bad and memorization is a four-letter word. Students are supposed to do 'higher-level' thinking about things they know nothing about.

One outspoken critic stated: "Bloom's Taxonomy is a serious impediment to education in America. It needs to be uprooted and eradicated if we want to educate children in a way that actually works…[T]ypical Evaluation questions take the form of 'What do you think about X?' and 'Do you agree with X?' These questions are often accompanied by praise for what education literature misidentifies as the 'Socratic Method.' The result of this strategy is to occupy class time with vacuous opining."

This critic points out that, "In Book VII of his *Republic*, Plato said that real higher order education—education into what he called the dialectic—couldn't start until the student… had mastered conventional wisdom."

Finding that my instincts align with Plato has prompted me to present Price's Taxonomy. It has only two steps: 1) teach kids lots of information; 2) teach kids to compare, explain, prioritize, and make deductions from that information.

Historically, every teacher knew that the real game was geography, history, science, the arts, etc. Kids learned thousands of facts in elementary and middle school, and in the process they learned how to manipulate information. At that point, children are engaged in higher-order thinking.

Most of what public schools chatter about is nonsense. As the outspoken critic summed up his views: "The Taxonomy, in its call for higher order thinking, has become a tool for subverting the transmission of knowledge."

Bloom's Taxonomy illustrates a phenomenon I call pretend-precision. What after all is the difference between "understanding facts" and "analyzing facts"? Teachers in training, and indeed entire school systems, are kept busy trying to understand pointless distinctions like that.

Basic problem: the Education Establishment is knowledge-averse. This is a serious psychological condition that often leads to blooming idiocy.

6. COMMON CORE ENSHRINES THE WORST

That's how you know the commissars aren't sincere. If they were sincere, they would create good methods.

Education That You Know Is Sick

Common Core claims to raise standards. In practice, it's psychological assault and battery. Kids get dumber and more depressed.

Headline on Daily Caller complains: "Principals say Common Core tests make little kids vomit, pee their pants."

Top comedian Louis C.K. shook the educational world with this tweet: "My kids used to love math. Now it makes them cry." Louis C.K. blamed Common Core.

Twitchy.com ran this headline: "What is Common Core doing to America's children? Mom shares heartrending photo."

The mother explains: "This is my middle child in the photo … She is 7 and is in 2nd grade…After checking her work, I had found 2 math problems were incorrect. I tried to help her understand where she went wrong but I don't understand it myself and was not much help.…I told her to forget about it and we'd try again tomorrow but she became very upset that she could not get the answer and kept trying and trying to fix it. She is hard on herself as she very much wants to excel in school… This is first photo of her that I have ever hated."

How do our professors work this sick magic? The basic technique is to create garbled problems that have no clear answer. Here is a hypothetical illustration of the basic gimmick: "Tom has six oranges. Mary has five oranges. Mrs. Smith has ten oranges. How many pies can they make?"

The average adult says, hey, wait a minute, that's bull. The average child, however, assumes you are asking an honest question; and grows increasingly miserable trying to answer it. Furthermore, that example is obviously silly; many others used in schools will defeat most adults.

For example, this problem has puzzled a multitude: "Tyler made 36 total snowflakes which is a multiple of how triangular snowflakes he made. How many triangular snowflakes could he have made?"

It seems to have a typo or two but even if you can fix that, will you be any closer to an answer?

Here's one that is short and slippery: "A gymnastic meet is 2 hours long. It has 8 competitors and each competes in 4 events. How many events will be scored?"

Does this actually have an answer? What is the impact of mentioning "2 hours"? In any case, are there hacks in our Department of Education who claim that one child in ten can confidently answer this? So why would it be used?

Now we come to what has been hailed as the worst question ever:

"Juanita wants to give bags of stickers to her friends. She wants to give the same number of stickers to each friend. She's not sure if she needs 4 bags or 6 bags of stickers. How many stickers could she buy so there are no stickers left over?"

My nephew, a math major, insisted the answer is obvious. I said he might know the answer but don't tell me it's obvious. Later I found out that Twitchy readers were invited to solve the question and they agreed that the answer is either 12, 24, 0, or 7. Obviously.

Now, all this sick fruit suggests a sick tree. That would be our Education Establishment. These ideologues seem to be in pursuit of a society so disoriented it will let them be in charge.

It's interesting that the only reason we are talking about these ideologues is that they have gone too far. They have created questions so perverse that lots of people are alarmed.

Why would our ideologues give away their game by creating these elusive math problems? First, I think they are desperate to move quickly. They want children dumbed today, not in a few years. Secondly, it's clear they think they can get away with it. (They probably assumed that Hillary Clinton would win the election and continue Obama's policies.)

A lot of what goes on in our public schools has a distinct odor of disdain and arrogance. "In your face, peasants. Do not oppose us. We are Alphas and you are sewer workers."

The part that is not so obvious is that this game has been played

**continuously for more than 60 years. New Math, in development
for many years, came and went in five years circa 1965. But today's
essential gimmick was fully developed at that time. You take stuff
that is normally done in college, drop it into the second grade, and
you have a kid-wrecker.**

"Topics introduced in the New Math include modular arithmetic,
algebraic inequalities, matrices, symbolic logic, Boolean algebra, and
abstract algebra."

According to one account "Parents were...vocal in their
opposition, claiming that they couldn't help their third-graders with
their homework anymore, and pointed to a noticeable decline in the
more concrete skills such as computation."

New Math was derided in the public forum. Morris Kline, in *Why
Johnny Can't Add: The Failure of the New Math* [1973], wrote that 'with
near perfect regularity, [teachers] applaud the return to traditional
content and instructional methods, and higher standards of student
performance.'"

This was a bitter defeat for our Progressives. Parents wanted their
children to learn basic arithmetic. What impertinence. The answer was
to lay low for a decade, put together a coalition of fancy-name front
groups, and come roaring back with Reform Math. Same pig, new
wardrobe.

Instead of one sick curriculum that everyone would have to deal
with, the professors created a dozen dysfunctional curricula so that
resistance would be divided, and futile.

Reform Math is what parents are still dealing with in Common
Core, particularly the curriculum called Everyday Math. There are
whole websites devoted to hating EM.

Don't imagine that math instruction is an isolated phenomenon
and thus possibly an accident. Everyday Math is comparable to non-
phonetic methods used to teach reading.

**In essence, here is the formula used throughout public schools,
in every subject. Find a technique that pretends to teach something
but doesn't. I say this is sick instruction, devised by sick people, on
behalf of sick goals.**

The people behind this are the same sort who invented Death
Education (a/k/a "values clarification") in the 1950s. This is where
young children have to answer morbid hypotheticals. A lifeboat will
hold only six people. Your family has eight members. Who must

drown? Clearly, our experts have been making kids sick for a long time.

Throughout all this bad education, you see the imprint of Russian psychology and particularly Pavlovian psychology. The goal was always to figure out how to control people, shape people, shock people, or make them surrender more quickly. The Russians love the idea of tricking you into defeat. And that's what Common Core seems intended to do.

Call the whole thing subversion, or treachery, or greed, or psychopathology, but please don't call it education.

I'm indebted to *The Cult of Common Core*, a fine book by Brad McQueen, for this money quote: "I have gotten to know a very different Bill Gates as I dug into the cult of Common Core. Now I see him as that creepy old man sitting alone at the edge of the playground with his hands in his pockets asking kids if they want some Common Core candy."

———

Affordable Care Act and Common Core—Both Are Bad to the Bone

Medical insurance and public education might seem to be two different worlds with different problems. But the proposed solutions were essentially the same. Here are ten descriptions that apply equally to ObamaCare and Common Core:

1) HUGE FEDERAL POWER GRAB: The obvious result from both programs is that Obama and his Czars got a bigger government to administer, more money to play with, more jobs for their loyal troops, and more control over people's lives.

2) NOT A RESPONSE TO POPULAR DEMAND: Both programs were massive, top-down interventions demanded by leftwing politics and ideology, not something the public asked for. Alleged problems were used as an excuse for adopting solutions that would grow government. The big question was, what can they get away with?

3) INCOMPREHENSIBLE BY DESIGN: A sentence was not used if a paragraph could be concocted. Thousands of new requirements, regulations, laws, and standards were contained in dense verbiage that neither Congress nor public would ever read and couldn't understand if they did. Almost every paragraph includes expanded powers and hidden consequences. Citizens would be further reduced to a childlike dependence on bureaucrats.

4) PUBLIC EXCLUDED FROM LEGISLATIVE PROCESS: The complexity of the political process, plus the density of jargon and propaganda, ensured that John Q Citizen was ignored. These programs were passed by stealth, chicanery, arm-twisting, and bribes. The Cornhusker Kickback put ObamaCare over the top. Similarly, so-called stimulus money earmarked for shovel-ready jobs was used as grants (i.e. bribes) to persuade the states to embrace Race to the Top, a precursor of Common Core. The fix was in.

5) DISHONEST MARKETING: The Obama administration made endless promises that turned out to be endless lies, all symbolized by Obama's promise that if you like your plan, you can keep your plan. States were told that if they liked their schools the way they are, they can keep them that way. In fact, these programs require changing everything.

6) MEDIA COMPLICIT: The mainstream media became cheerleaders. News reports were not critical or analytical. Try to find a newspaper in America which opposed these radical programs. The average local paper wrote editorial after editorial in support of ObamaCare and Common Core.

7) VERY EXPENSIVE AND WOULD GET MORE SO: Propaganda for these programs emphasized that the government would save money and individual citizens would get more for less. In fact, medical costs immediately went up for individuals, as did the outlays to implement Common Core. Improvement, if any, will be negligible, not that improvement was ever the primary goal.

8) FUNDAMENTAL TRANSFORMATION: Both programs embody what Obama meant when he talked about "a fundamental transformation of the country." Translation: his socialist way or the highway. Socialists have been seeking this "transformation" for more than 100 years.

9) TOTALITARIAN INTENT: Both programs prescribed in detail how everyone must think and behave. Both programs allow the government to collect far more information and to meddle in more aspects of everyone's life. It was like giving the EPA two more sectors to regulate.

10) INSTANT TRAIN WRECKS: Both programs, once they left the station, became train wrecks. of course it was too late by that time to stop them. As things continue to go wrong, bureaucracies will simply declare: "It's a big success. Everything is just like we planned." Yes, that might, grimly enough, be exactly true.

All the similarities mean that once you understand one of these things, you understand the other. They are two facets on the same zirconium. They are two fronts of the same coup.

There is a miasma of fraud, malfeasance, and bad faith hanging over both these schemes. The logical thing for the country is to repeal both, or get ready for the worst.

QED: Socialists have the same answer for every problem: a huge and vastly expensive new government program.

———

A Cruel Hoax: "Obama Vows to Improve Education at All Levels"

An AP story about Obama and education appeared in scores of American newspapers (during 2014).

According to the report, "President Barack Obama is promising to improve American education from preschool to college."

The story appeared as there was a drumbeat for pre-K (or "quality pre-K" as the ever-sycophantic New York Times puts it). One problem: if K-12 classrooms are wracked by mediocrity now, why is pre-K, or anything else, suddenly going to be conducted at a high level? That would be most unlikely. Here's why:

In his State of the Union, Obama made a laundry list of promises.

Some of them are concerned with technology and grants. These he might be able to fulfill.

But the promise of improving education at all levels is mocked by the fact that Common Core, his signature effort in this area, is now devastating education at all levels in all states that have embraced it.

Simultaneously with the AP story, there was a new Breitbart story about Governor Huckabee backtracking on his support for Common Core. Apparently his fans and supporters screamed and booed at such volume that Huckabee had to pay attention. His new line was that he's in favor of it but he isn't: he wants some new terminology; he wants rebranding, as if that would change the nature of the beast. Indeed, many states are now changing the jargon. **This is precisely what our Education Establishment has always done. As soon as the public discovers that a new idea is a bad idea, our education experts don't change the idea, they change the names.**

Common Core was never something the public asked for. It was schemed and dreamed by the Education Establishment. It became a reality only because Obama had "stimulus money" that he could channel into grants (in effect, bribes) for semi-bankrupt states circa 2009. Lots of glorious excuses and rhetoric were thrown at the country to make this hot-air balloon fly. Many intelligent people such as Huckabee supported it. Many people who should know better, such as the business community, supported it. Many liberal newspapers, to no one's surprise, supported it in their usual slavish fashion. So for a few years there was a genuine Common Core tsunami flooding across the country.

Then individual citizens learned what was inside this thing. They realized, for one thing, it was an exact parallel with ObamaCare. A huge overreach by the federal government, packed with untested theories and methods, the whole thing sort of scaffolded up with popsicle sticks.

As famed educator Siegfried Engelmann explained: "Common Core is a perfect example of technical nonsense. A sensible organization would rely heavily on data about procedures used to achieve outstanding results; and they would certainly field test the results to assure that the standards resulted in fair, achievable goals? How many of these things did they do? None."

The essential problem with Common Core is that there's nothing new. It's really a repackaging of all the bad ideas that John Dewey and his progressive educators came up with in the last 80 or 90 years. The basic idea is to teach children less because that's considered to be fairer. Johnny can't feel superior to Jack if neither one knows very much. Now, this approach may lead you to socialism but it will definitely not lead you to an educated country.

So President Obama's lofty claims in his State of the Union speech were obliterated by what is actually happening in K-12 education in most cities in America. Charlotte Iserbyt's famous phrase "the deliberate dumbing down of America" seems more apt than ever.

The paradox we see in education is the same as that in the economy. The president talks about progress and success but his political philosophy mitigates against success. Success would mean that rich people would get richer in some cases, and it would mean that smart people learn a lot more in some cases. And we can't have those outcomes. Indeed, they are carefully prevented. So Obama's rhetoric notwithstanding, his policies lead to intellectual and economic stagnation.

As Robin Eubanks asserts in *Credentialed to Destroy*: "What is being marketed as the Common Core national standards and accompanying ed reforms is actually a planned, centrally coordinated, interrelated, complete reorganization of American education. Designed to change students from the inside-out so they will lobby for social change now. And vote for it later. These so-called `reforms' eliminate practices, like the transmission curriculum, that evolved because they worked and created prosperous practices and useful, marketable knowledge and skills. And a spirit of individualism that has created great innovations... Common Core would be a bad idea if the intentions of its planners were for the best. But they are not."

"Close Reading" Is Close to a Con

A key component of the Common Core blitzkrieg is something called "close reading." Thanks to this pedagogical marvel, we are assured, kids who can hardly read will now read deeply.

"Close reading" is not a new term. "The technique as practiced today was pioneered (at least in English) by I. A. Richards and his student William Empson, later developed further by the New Critics of the mid-twentieth century...Close reading describes, in literary criticism, the careful, sustained interpretation of a brief passage of text," according to Wikipedia.

College students majoring in English Literature know they must try to dive deep into famous works of fiction and nonfiction. of course, at that point in their lives, the students have read 50 books, probably 250. They are fast, relaxed readers. The surface of the text is like the surface of a lake for a powerful swimmer. These people are ready to plunge to deeper levels.

Hold on, says the Education Establishment. "[C]lose reading can't wait until 7th grade or junior year in high school. It needs to find its niche in kindergarten and the years just beyond if we mean to build the habits of mind that will lead all students to deep understanding of text," according to ASCD (Association for Supervision and Curriculum Development).

Caution: now entering an alternative reality.

A serious problem at this point is that more than half our fourth graders are not proficient readers Same with our eighth graders. You cannot expect these children to do "close reading" because they cannot, in any real sense, do "reading."

Let's pause for a moment and consider what should be going on. Reading is like learning to ride a bike. You have to be on the bike for many hours, riding over streets, grass, and curbs, until you are comfortable and riding for pleasure.

Children in elementary and middle school need quantity, not quality. Schools should use every trick to seduce children into reading LOTS of books. Such books do not need depth. It's enough that they have a good story or engaging information, and that children say, "That was fun. I want to read another one."

For hundreds of years, there were books written especially for children, for example, the Hardy Boys or the Bobbsey Twins. Children who are devouring such books at a rapid rate can be encouraged to read more complex texts, and to read them more deeply. Unfortunately, such readers are now the exceptions.

Many Americans, even college graduates, never reach the level of reading for fun. Millions can read in some technical sense, but the whole process is hard work. They do it on the job, if they have to.

NPR's "All Things Considered" reported: "Fewer and fewer Americans are reading for pleasure. That's the conclusion of a study released today by the National Endowment for the Arts. It tracks a decline among Americans of all ages. Here are a couple of the most striking statistics. On average, Americans spend two hours a day watching television and seven minutes reading. And only one-third of 13-year-olds are daily readers."

But now, thanks to the genius of Common Core, children who may not have finished one actual book, will be parsing and analyzing like a literary critic at the New York Times.

According to a Common Core website "Essentially, close reading means reading to uncover layers of meaning that lead to deep comprehension. Close, analytic reading stresses engaging with a text of sufficient complexity directly and examining meaning thoroughly and methodically, encouraging students to read and reread deliberately. Directing student attention on the text itself empowers students to understand the central ideas and key supporting details."

This is patently unlikely for average kids. Their pulses will not quicken. A lot of this "deep comprehension" sounds boring even for literary types. Kids will never know that literature was created to be entertainment.

Some of the recommended texts are clearly not what students in elementary or middle school would curl up with on a rainy day: speeches by Martin Luther King, a Shakespearean play, and the Constitution.

David Coleman, master of the Common Core and characterized as one of the "Ten Scariest People in Education," has launched a crusade against literature and narrative. Instead, he wants children to marinate in dreary, informational text.

Males especially will suspect that "close reading" is merely another chapter in the war against boys. Coleman embraces insulation installation manuals, presidential executive orders, environmental programming, and federal reserve documents. In short, tough dull text, probably with a PC spin. But in the real world, people read for story and beauty, or hardly at all. Dramatic stories are how we draw young people inside books.

There is also the question of culture, as in a shared experience. Who would want to share the fatuous, acultural experiences that Coleman is foisting on the schools?

One recalls that in New Math, children were supposed to learn matrices, Boolean algebra, and base-8. What could be the purpose of this absurd leap into adult academic activities? For one thing, it probably intimidates parents. Are they going to admit they don't know what Boolean algebra is?

Close Reading seems to me like teaching Boolean algebra to fourth graders, pretentious and inane. New Math did not teach math. It's a safe prediction that Close Reading will not teach reading.

In sports, if you take children up an expert slope and turn them loose, you may end up in jail. But in education you can put children in an uncomfortable hopeless situation, where they can never really succeed, and you get a grant or a promotion.

Here's more shtick on an education website: "Reading Packs provide teachers with a resource that promotes careful analysis of text while building 21st Century skills of critical thinking, collaboration, and communication. Students contemplate a Key Question as they participate in self-directed, small-group, and whole-class discussion following their independent reading of engaging passages on a common topic...The Teaching Tips also provide teachers with pointers for serving as discussion facilitators as they help students reach consensus on their answer to the Key Question."

Notice the phrases "small group and whole class discussion" leading to "consensus." It's possible that children murmur and stumble through text as part of a group but never engage in anything legitimately called close or deep reading.

So, we are told, the walking wounded of the typical public school will be led to the literary promised land. People who cannot read a few paragraphs out of the newspaper without major mistakes will magically become college and career ready, thanks to Close Reading.

Isn't this just too creepy and unrealistic to be taken seriously? Alas no. Common Core, as described earlier, is a blitzkrieg, a massive 2000-mile front advancing across the United States, twisting arms and throwing cash in all directions.

———

Why "Align" Is Malign

Once upon a time, a teacher would teach American History. On exams, students would be asked questions about American History. Testing was straightforward and needed little discussion.

In the modern era, however, content is disparaged and facts are scorned. The goal, seemingly, is to keep kids busy but to teach as little as possible.

The big problem is, how do you design exams when the teacher hasn't taught much, the kids don't know much, and there is little actual knowledge that the school intends the children to retain?

In this fact-free world, what would a valid examination look like?

At this moment, thousands of the smartest people in education are sitting around tables trying to design "authentic assessment." Experts must somehow "align" testing with diminished content. Professors of education must prepare a testing regime which continues through the year. But finally nothing very substantial is actually taught or tested.

Aligning a triangle with a circle is difficult. Aligning a triangle with smoke rings is converging on impossible. What's the answer?

Hype and self-congratulation, for starters.

Be ready. You are going to hear such a tsunami of claims about the new assessments and how they are so perfectly aligned. You will feel that you're in Biblical times and that God has once again written his wishes on slabs of rock.

Here's how the plot has so far unfolded. The first order of business is to shift emphasis from what students know to what they know how to do (or what they feel). In schools 100 years ago, it was assumed that you knew how to sharpen a pencil, go to the library, use a dictionary, write an essay, engage in research, or tackle a science project. These were tools that allowed you to do the actual work. Not worth talking about.

The trick now is to turn the game upside down. What students know is fading into irrelevance. What they know how to do is what matters. What process, what procedure, what activity, can you be tested on?

More and more the emphasis is on such questions as: Can you work with others? Can you be creative? Can you compare and contrast two objects? (That's called critical thinking.) Can you network? Can you use the internet? Can you prepare a PowerPoint presentation. Ergo, schools must devise tests that measure *those things*. That's called "alignment."

You won't be asked questions about the Civil War or any actual war. You might be asked about a theoretical war. For example, you might be asked for advice on Civil Defense and protecting the water supply. How would you set about preparing a report?

All the way back in John Dewey's time, the Education Establishment wanted to give more importance to "activities." By mid-20th century, the emphasis was on real-life skills. At that point, things were still easy for the Education Establishment. They taught you how to use the subway to go to work. On the exam they would ask you how you might go to work. Things were still aligned!

The problem is that the parents, colleges, and employers kept insisting that children learn knowledge. Schools were put in the position of pretending to teach something, anything.

We are moving toward the Common Core Curriculum. You will hear many pretentious claims of higher "standards." Stating a hifalutin standard does not mean anyone actually reaches it. Meanwhile, there is the urgent need to create tests that will make it seem as though traditional educational patterns are being replaced by something better.

The cry, again and again, is for "authentic assessment." Experts must develop ingenious new tests to measure the wonderful new things we are teaching. No one is going to admit how very little that is. Educators, the ones who expect to be promoted in any case, will not let that thought into their heads. They will insist that we have entered a new era. In a way they are right.

How will you sort out what is really happening? Easy.

Look in the Yellow Pages. You can probably find hundreds of schools. Beauty. Driving. Bartending. Martial arts. Flower arranging. Acupuncture. Investing. Nursing. Painting. Photography. Language. Mountain climbing. Swimming. Juggling. Acting. In a big city there might be hundreds of different kinds of schools. In one important way they are identical.

Every real school possesses a body of knowledge, which it teaches to students. Along the way the students are tested. At the end of the course, students earn a certificate stating that they now possess that body of knowledge. If they don't, they can sue. That's the paradigm we're losing. The Education Establishment hates this

paradigm.

What's happening is close to a scam. All this chatter about alignment tells you that the public schools are not serious about teaching content. If they were, the old tests would work fine. We need new assessments because something new is going on. You might read a list of things that are taught. Look closely. They will all be attitudes and activities. You will not see a name, date, place, or fact. That's how you know that it's not a real school as traditionally understood.

When public schools are again teaching a body of knowledge, they'll be real schools. You'll hear no talk of alignment or authentic assessment. Until then, they'll be faking it.

————

Common Core's Dirtiest Trick: Dividing Parents and Children

When you look back at New Math (ca. 1965) and Reform Math (ca. 1990), one of the most striking and persistent features was that parents could not understand the homework which their children brought home.

Mystified parents were trying to advise mystified children. The parents, presumably the wise members of the society, were helpless to say anything useful when confronted by the weird complexities of "reform" math, which has now been rolled forward into Common Core.

Here is a commonplace horror story that can stand in for millions of others: "When Mike and Camille Chudzinski tried to help their son with his homework earlier this fall, they were bewildered. The fourth-grader brought home no spelling lists, few textbooks, and a whole new approach to solving math problems. When he tackled multi-digit addition, for instance, Patrick did not just line up the two numbers and then add the columns, as his parents had been taught to do. Instead, he sketched out a graph with a series of arrows and marks that appeared at first to his parents as indecipherable as hieroglyphics."

When we hear these stories, we typically focus on the comical oddity of adults not being able to do homework intended for children. How is that even possible? But the ramifications are anything but funny.

The real damage is that Reform Math opens up fractures throughout society Parents are cut off from their children. Parents and schools are pitted against each other. Students are alienated from their teachers and schools.

Sociologist James Coleman said that the most important thing in successful education is what he called "social capital." Ideally, parents, kids, schools, and community are on the same page, working toward the same goals. In this way the children feel they are doing appropriate and necessary work. Energy is used to complete tasks, not to debate the merits of the tasks.

Imagine the situation in Reform Math when parents can't do even elementary problems in arithmetic. Adults are angry; children are stressed. Parents have conferences with teachers, and complain later in front of the children that the teachers couldn't give them any satisfactory answers. Why would children be enthusiastic about mastering something that their own parents find impossible and reprehensible?

All of this tension and hostility adds up to the perfect excuse for the child to lose interest in math, and in school generally. We hear lots of stories about children who are miserable at school. We shouldn't be surprised.

In short, Reform Math is not just bad because it doesn't teach math, it's bad because it's a society-wrecker. This is Common Core's dirtiest trick.

In an intelligently organized society, the schools would do everything possible to involve parents in their children's education. Our Education Establishment is doing the reverse. Schools seem intent on making parents turn their backs on their children's education.

Driving parents out of the equation means driving education out of the equation.

Today, whenever schools are not getting good results, the first excuse the Education Establishment offers is that parents don't want to help. This is diabolical. The schools do everything possible to make parents give up on education, and then the schools blame the parents.

Professor Michael Toscano writes: "Educational success is also dependent upon closure between families and their schools. In the case of the CCSS, little real 'social capital' exists between parents and schools, because the standards were adopted out of the reach of parents and because they will remain out of their reach. This is a crucial mistake. Education must be a common good that emanates from the relations of families in a community."

When New Math was first introduced 60 years ago and parents complained, the official propaganda was that the new methods were so sophisticated, parents simply weren't ready for them. Many in the community accepted the claim that children would finally benefit from being pushed in this way. That was a mistake. New Math was, for all practical purposes, irrational. It soon self-destructed and then we knew that it, not parents, had been flawed all along. This pattern continues. The community should use a common-sense "smell test." School work too complicated for parents is too complicated, period. It's not appropriate for children.

Common Core has embraced and recycled all the worst ideas from "reform" math. One has to conclude that the people responsible are hopelessly incompetent or hopelessly ideological.

The more you reflect on the flood of horror stories, the more you feel that Common Core commissars must spend their time concocting ways to alienate children and defeat parents. The basic taunt seems to be: "Hey, you parents. You can gripe and complain and thereby look foolish in the eyes of your children; or you can cower in surrender as you learn to put up with the artificial nonsense that we have devised, thanks to millions in grant from the government (your taxes used against you). *Haha, suckers. You can't win.* Obama promised a fundamental transformation and the first thing we're going to transform is your sense of importance as parents. You must learn that you are insignificant."

The divide between parents and children is a far more critical issue than many imagine. The proper priority is that homework should be specifically designed to bring parents and children together. Common Core seems cunningly designed to do the opposite. That's the main reason it must be defeated.

QED: Common Core is a pedagogical failure. But it is successful at making society dysfunctional.

7. LITERARY FLIGHTS

**Who says serious has to be boring?
Besides, some of this stuff is so grim, you need to laugh.**

Education: Waiting for Lewis Black

According to a movie and book that came out in 2010, everyone is *Waiting for Superman*.

That would be the heroic, miraculous, too-good-to-be-true person who will swoop down into even the worst neighborhoods and rescue all those bad-luck kids.

Me, I'm not counting on Superman. Public schools are too weird. The Man of Steel will look foolish fighting to the death against silly putty.

To speak truth about this demented demimonde, we need a voice, a mind, a way of thinking as deranged as the system itself.

We need Lewis Black. You know him, of course. He's the quintessential angry comic. On stage he appears to be having a seizure. His hands tremble upward in gestures of helpless rage. Spit seems to fly from his mouth as he hurls bombs made of bitterness. It's easy to imagine him chomping off these insults:

"KIDS CAN'T READ THEIR DIPLOMAS. THEY CAN'T FIND THIS COUNTRY ON A MAP. YOU'RE TEACHING THEM WHAT?? NO, YOU'RE TEACHING THEM NOTHING. YOU ARE KEEPING THEM EMPTY-HEADED. AND STUFFING THEM IN A DEEP HOLE AND PAVING IT OVER WITH ASPHALT MADE FROM CHOPPED UP ENCYCLOPEDIAS. AND WHAT'S THAT YOU'RE SAYING TO THEM?? BYE-BYE, SUCKERS!!!"

Here he might shake and shudder all over, a trademark gesture of disgust. Lewis Black—his style, his comedy, the way his mind functions—is the perfect counterpoint to the bogosity shown by our

Education Establishment. There are many thousands of these so-called experts, all gaudily festooned with degrees and titles. But Lewis Black could be their avenging-angel equal:

"YOU ASK ME, KIDS MUST KNOW THE NAMES of THE OCEANS. BUT NOOOO. OUR SUPERINTENDENTS AND PRINCIPALS ASK WHY, WHY WOULD CHILDREN NEED SUCH INFORMATION?? WELLLLL, HOW ABOUT BECAUSE THEY ARE HUMAN. THEY ARE ALIVE!!!!!!!. BECAUSE KIDS ARE NOT VEGETABLES. NOT TOMATOES GROWING ON A VINE. THEY ARE THE FUTURE of THE COUNTRY. AND THEY DON'T KNOW THE NAMES of THE OCEANS THAT WASH AGAINST OUR SHORES. BLAH-BLAH-BLANKETTY-BLAH."

Lewis Black doesn't look healthy. He's been on dark journeys to hell and back. He probably smokes and drinks too much. His mind has been poked and strobed by too many titanically terrible experiences. But now he's back from the dread, to tell us the low-down on our intellectual slow-down:

"THIS BOY IS IN COLLEGE. HE'S IN A FRATERNITY. HE HAS A DRIVER'S LICENSE AND OWNS A CAR AND CAN VOTE. BUT HE CAN'T TELL YOU WHAT 6 x 7 IS. WHERE'S A CALCULATOR??? HE'S IN SCHOOL 12 YEARS BEFORE COLLEGE. HE DOESN'T KNOW WHAT 6 X 7 IS! THINK ABOUT THIS FOR THREE SECONDS AND YOUR EYES WILL ROLL LIKE CHERRIES IN A SLOT MACHINE. SON-OF-A-BARBIE DOLL!"

Now his own eyes are rolling, side to side, then back in his head. Black will probably topple over and flatline on the stage. No, he rights himself as he gazes almost idiotically at the audience. Assembling, as if they were a giant jigsaw puzzle, his thoughts. His head twitches on an unsteady stalk. His whole body spasms with indignation, like some Manhattan cabbie cursing a dumb-ass tourist:

"I HAVE TO TELL YOU, ALL THIS CRAPADODDLEDO ABOUT HOW TO FIX THE SCHOOLS?...SOMEBODY IS LAUGHING AT YOU. THE KIDS CAN'T COUNT. THEY CAN'T READ. BUT SOMEHOW IT'S ALWAYS SOMEBODY ELSE'S FAULT. NOT THE PEOPLE RUNNING THE SCHOOLS. NOT ONE BIT. THEY JUST PULL ALL THE STRINGS, WRITE ALL THE LAWS, CREATE ALL THE POLICIES. BUT SOMEHOW

YOU KNOW WHOSE FAULT IT IS, SOME NICE WELFARE MOTHER IN QUEENS. IT'S ALL HER FAULT. IT'S SOME EIGHT-YEAR-OLD'S FAULT BECAUSE HE PLAYED A VIDEO GAME. SURE IT IS!"

Now Black is pacing like a tiger on meth, ten steps to our left, eight steps back the other way. Can he hold himself together? Will he explode like that can't-stop-eating guy in Monty Python? Bits and pieces of Lewis Black ten rows out, but people are screaming with joy?

"THESE KIDS CAN'T READ A CEREAL BOX. THEY CAN'T READ A SIGN ON THE STREET. WHO THE HECK IS IN CHARGE of READING??? THE ADDAMS FAMILY? F TROOP? PEOPLE WHO WANT TO PULL THE SWITCH ON DEATH ROW BUT CAN'T PASS THE IQ TEST??? WHO IS IN CHARGE of READING? TRUMP HAS A LOVE NOTE FOR YOU. READY? YOU'RE FIRED."

Now Black is making noises like a venting whale. Good, he's not exploding after all. *Oooops,* but he is going to projectile-vomit on the people in the front row. *Ohmiiigod...* At the last second he pulls back from the abyss and demands to know:

"IS IT THE FAULT of THE PARENTS? of COURSE IT IS! ESPECIALLY THOSE PARENTS WHO ARE GUILTY of WANTING THEIR KIDS TO KNOW HOW TO READ AND COUNT. THE UNGRATEFUL JERKS!!!! THEY DON'T APPRECIATE THE POINT of BEING DUMBED DOWN. THESE STUPID MIDDLEBROW PARENTS WANT THEIR KIDS TO KNOW THE NAMES of THE OCEANS. WHAT'S THE MATTER WITH THEM??"

Lewis Black is shaking all over, flinching, twisting, turning 180 degrees at a jerk. He advances to the front of the stage, a crazed Old Testament prophet. Surely he is going to put a curse on the world. It's the worst of times and the worst of times, and Black knows why:

"WHAT IS WRONG WITH YOU DUMB SCHMUCKS? THEY ARE PLAYING YOU FOR CHUMPS. THEY SHOWED YOU A CAR THAT WON'T RUN AND YOU BEGGED TO PAY $80,000 FOR IT. YOU'LL BE PAYING FOR IT UNTIL YOU DIE. YOUR KIDS WILL BE PAYING FOR IT UNTIL THEY DIE...

"I HEARD WE NEED VOLUNTEERS FOR A NEW COLONY ON MARS. I VOLUNTEER THE PEOPLE RUNNING OUR EDUCATION SYSTEM. OFF THEY GO! BYE-BYE! DON'T

BOTHER US ANYMORE. WE'LL LET YOU KNOW WHEN
YOU CAN COME BACK. GROUND CONTROL TO WORLD
CLASS TWITS. YOU WANT SOME MORE KIDS TO MESS UP,
FIND THEM ON MARS. HAHAHA."

(NB: this is satire. Black did not actually say these things.)

Education Establishment Are Great Pretenders

"Oh-oh, yes you are the great pretenders
Pretending that you're doing good
Your need is such that you pretend too much
You've done all the damage you could"

The top 1000 people in public education, let's call them the
Education Establishment. They make all the decisions. Our public
schools are what they are because of this tiny elite.

Some observers think these people are incompetent, clumsy,
addled. Maybe many are. But at the very top I suspect you find people
with total clarity. They know what they're doing. They know it's not
what most of the public wants. But they have an agenda, a collectivist
agenda, and they're not going to let anything get in their way.

If anyone points out that a great percent of children don't learn
to read, don't learn to do basic arithmetic, and don't know much basic
foundational information, at that point our elite educators become
great pretenders.

They insist they mean well. They insist that their every decision is
based on reams of research. They insist that everything is improving,
we merely need new kinds of assessment to show that.

They pretend that all of their progressive, modern, newfangled
approaches are the best. Give these people credit. They are some of the
finest hucksters in history.

**But finally, these people have to know the damage they are
doing. They have to know that their theories and pedagogies are
fake.** The paradigm for educational nonsense is called Whole Word.
You make children memorize English words as graphic designs; and

now we have 50 million functional illiterates. But that great damage is not the point at the moment. The point is that the nonsense-makers pretend not to know.

When New Math appeared in 1965, the American public, columnists, book reviewers, etc. agreed it was a disaster. In a few years, it disappeared from American life, despite being in development for more than 10 years. Do you think these Ph.D.'s accidentally designed the worst curriculum in history? It's more logical to assume they carefully designed the worst curriculum in history. When they got caught, they pretended they thought it was a great idea.

Move forward to 1985; the same gang brought out a whole new bunch of math curricula collectively called Reform Math, but sarcastically called New New Math, Voodoo Math, Fuzzy Math. There were actually 12 separate curricula, each with a dozen authors. That's a gigantic pile of Ph.D.'s but they came up with an incoherent and destructive mega-curriculum. Then they pretended to believe in it.

To fully appreciate how horrible Reform Math is, look at the discussions and debates that went on in many towns all across America when parent groups would rally against these things. And all the time the parents were complaining, the local representatives of the Education Establishment would blandly pretend that the program was very good if only people would give it a chance.

Maybe the low-level educators believe this. It is not possible the education elite believe this. (Professional mathematicians and other experts publicly denounced Reform Math.)

The next big gimmick was called Constructivism and this is where, instead of my telling you something, I tell you to go find out for yourself. Maybe it's a good technique for teaching a few special insights. But you have to set up these eureka moments; this takes time and patience. Typically, a good lecturer can communicate far more info in less time. Constructivism will be slow; and the material learned will be spotty. But the Education Establishment wants to pretend that this is actually a superior form of education, for all subjects and all ages.

So that's the perennial pattern. We are overrun by really bad ideas which naked emperors tell us are splendid, like their splendid clothes.

And every day in their offices, these professors look at the stats coming in from across the country and they know that their ideas are dumbing the country down. They pretend to be concerned. They pretend to be working on the next generation of curricula,

that will be so much better than the junk they confected 10 years ago.

As best I can understand it, being in the Education Establishment is like being a priest in a religion. You have to embrace church dogma, totally. But finally the tenets of a church come back to faith. Then we're talking about God, infinity, and complex things that you can't check out personally. But the gizmos that our Education Establishment promotes are not of this rarefied variety. These bad ideas are in the classroom. You can see they are goofy and don't work. You can measure the bad results.

So you know the elite educators are pretending. They know they're pretending.

> *"Oh-oh, yes you are the great pretenders*
> *Adrift in a world of your own*
> *You've upped your game and to our real shame*
> *You've nibbled us down to the bone"*

———

"You Don't Need No Education!"

In Pink Floyd's *Another Brick in the Wall Part 2* we heard, circa 1980, one of the most famous lines in all of rock 'n roll: "We don't need no education."

It was a countercultural time. This was meant to be the angry voice of adolescent angst and rebellion.

In fact, few teenagers ever articulate the extreme thought that they don't need school. They may not like the teachers, the subjects, the way they are taught, oh, lots of things. But that's not the same as saying they don't want an education. Most teenagers know they need an education. *If only the schools would provide one.*

How strange the world has become. In the US, it's not the children crying out against education. It's the people in charge of education crying out against education. This has to be one of the most remarkable role reversals in history.

John Dewey is always credited with being the Father of American

Education. Unfortunately, he is. Dewey was a collectivist, i.e., a leveler. His writings bristle with hostility to traditional academic pursuits. He said (1899): "The mere absorbing of facts and truths...tends very naturally to pass into selfishness. There is no obvious social motive for the acquirement of mere learning." *Mere?*

Dewey wrote: "I believe that this educational process has two sides—one psychological and one sociological." Parse that all day and you won't find any mention of the side where children actually learn something.

Dewey drew up the blueprint for progressive (actually, regressive) education. Our so-called professors of education still follow it today. The entire message can be summarized in five words: "YOU don't need no education!"

That's what our Education Establishment, in dozens of formulations and catchy jargon, is telling the children in public schools: "You don't need no education!"

Teachers make it clear that basic skills and knowledge are not worth bothering with. It's a waste of time to memorize the multiplication tables or where countries are on a map. No, there's nothing subtle about it. Students know what the school is preaching: "YOU don't need no education!"

Should children bother learning dates, facts, foundational information? of course not. No one will be expected to memorize anything. Not only that, the teachers will not try to teach much of anything. Students will be encouraged to acquire such knowledge as they can "construct" for themselves. Perhaps the message was subtle 50 years ago. But now the schools are screaming it: "You don't need no education!"

The student are not dumb. They understand their marching orders from the first grade onward. Reading is taught in a way that can't work (memorizing Sight-Words). Arithmetic is taught by a fuzzy, incoherent method that bounces from topic to topic. Children don't master basic skills. Teachers go through the motions of teaching but the broader message fills the air: "You don't need no education!"

The system is designed to move students to a high school diploma and a place in college, even if they don't know enough to be there. Assessments are "authentic," i.e., tests are easy and answers can be fuzzy. Almost everyone gets an A. Cheating is overlooked and excused. Bad grammar and misspellings are considered trivial. There is nobody saying, "Work hard. You need to learn this material." All the voices are saying the opposite: "You don't need no education!"

What an irony. The Education Establishment would be more properly called the Anti-Education Establishment. They seem to think it's their job to dumb down the schools, the students, the culture, the entire society. As long as John Dewey's collectivist philosophy controls education, education will be impoverished and inane.

CODA: This debate is especially important now when Common Core Curriculum has descended upon the country.

If schools were run by people who really cared about education, maybe it wouldn't be so bad to give more control to the federal government. But Common Core Curriculum seems to be a euphemism for all the worst ideas from the past 80 years. The elite educators will make sure your kids learn close to nothing, even as everyone chatters on about 21st-century skills, student-centered learning, creativity, cooperation, standards-based education, competency-based education, and all the rest.

But in practice children will reach the age of 20 not knowing where Japan is on a map, what 7 x 8 is, and no clear picture of what goes around what when sun, moon, and earth are discussed.

Actions, they say, speak louder than words. Whatever the Education Establishment is saying, their actions are screaming: "You don't need no education. And we don't intend to give you one."

———

Education Establishment Skillful at One Thing: Ignorance

The *Washington Post* recently reported: "SAT reading scores for graduating high school seniors this year reached the lowest point in nearly four decades."

As reading goes, so goes education generally.

Let me sum this up. Americans get dumber ever year in every subject. People do not know even the simple stuff. You don't need SAT scores to tell you this. Every time Jay Leno went *Jaywalking*, he chronicled our steady decline. (Mark Dice and Jesse Watters now do similar man-in-the-street videos.)

Bottom line, when you read in the media that our top-level educators are deeply concerned with Learning, Achievement, Higher-Level Thinking, Critical Thinking, Cognitive Skills, and other high-sounding phrases, the proper reaction is: *piffle*. These people are good at only one thing; making sure their students are not well informed.

Americans don't know very much for the obvious reason that public schools refuse to teach very much. Yes, they refuse. When you look at YouTube videos and assess the sort of EASY, low-level knowledge that people do not know, you can reach only one conclusion: our Education Establishment is hostile to education as this term was once understood? That hostility is killing us. **Take care of basic skills and basic knowledge, and everything else will fall into place. Unfortunately, our Education Establishment has spent decades building a fact-free school. Kids are kept busy all day but they are not expected to learn a lot.**

As you read the following typical examples taken from several Jay Leno episodes, note two fascinating aspects. First, many people haven't learned much. Second, they confidently throw out any little facts they do know. Educated people know what they don't know; these people do not. Apparently, they've been trained to GUESS at everything. Reading, math, history, geography–there are no solid facts, only a mush one reaches into, hoping to get lucky.

"Who was president during the First World War?"
"Eisenhower?"

"When did Columbus discover America?"
"1842?"

"What separates your inner ear from your outer ear?"
"Your brain."

"The seven land masses on Earth are called what?"
"A lake?"

"People who live in Appalachia are from what country?"
"Sweden."

"Who did we get our independence from?"
"Thomas Jefferson."

"When was the Depression?"
"Late 1800s."

"Guantanamo Bay is in what country?"
"I wanna say Asia."

"How many stars on the flag?"
"32."

"Where is the Alamo?"
"London?"

"Blessed are the meek for they shall…?"
"Eat."

"How long ago did Jesus live?"
"Two hundred and fifty million years."

"How many justices on the Supreme Court?"
A young attorney guessed: "Twelve…Nine?…Twelve?"

"Who were Lewis and Clark?"
"Superman and…?"

"How about Bush 41?"
"Is it a drink?"

"When was Pearl Harbor?"
"It was…like 1967…The Chinese people invaded America."

"Who said 'Give me liberty or give me death'?"
"Bonaparte."

"Whose face is on the one dollar bill?"
"Somebody famous."

"Who warned that the British were coming?"
"The Confederates."

"What two animals are the symbols of the stock market?"
"The snake and the mouse."

"Who elects Congress?"
"The President?"

"What country did we fight in the American Revolutionary War?"
"France?"

"How long ago was Jesus born?"
"I'd say four hundred years."

"In what month do we vote for presidents?"
"October?… September?"

"Who wrote our national anthem?"
A history teacher guessed: "Somebody B. Scott?"

"If you're Parisian, what nationality are you?"
"You live in Peru."

"What year was Independence Day?"
"July 4th, 1864."

"Where do they speak Gaelic?"
"San Francisco."

"Egypt is located on what continent?"
"South America."

"What two sides fought in the American Civil War?"
"Germany."

"What is the name of our national anthem?"
"I pledge allegiance to the flag…"

"Who landed at Plymouth Rock?"
"The Mayflower, the Pinto and the Santa Maria."

It's easy to see that our Education Establishment has been very ingenious at coming up with techniques for watering-down and dumbing-down. The part I can't figure out is why do Americans put up with this malfeasance?

Why doesn't the Republican Party make education a BIG issue? Why doesn't every local election turn on who will improve the schools? Why don't military and business leaders put loud and relentless pressure on the schools to do a better job? Why doesn't every newspaper in the country raise a ruckus about dumb schools? (Newspapers need readers. Where is it written that newspapers have to conspire in their own destruction?) Why aren't people yelling: we're mad as hell and we won't take it anymore? Meanwhile, the Education Establishment goes blandly on, playing undertaker to American civilization. If these people were as good at teaching as they are at non-teaching, we would have a new Golden Age.

A Funny Thing Happened in School Today

A funny thing happened in school today. Not funny *ha-ha* but funny as in bizarre and unexpected. Funny as in funny money.

And not just today. Yesterday. Tomorrow. Every day. Every time a school teaches reading in a way that doesn't work. That's funny, right? You teach reading but nobody learns to read.

And not just in any one school. No, this epic lack of progress is happening everywhere. Point to a school and you're probably looking at a dead zone literacy-wise.

A school's first job is to teach kids to read. But somehow our schools have figured out sure-fire ways to make sure children never master this essential skill. Now that's funny. Like a guy slipping on a banana peel and breaking his leg.

So here we are with 50 million people possessing only marginal literacy. Every day our schools turn out more.

Kids have been learning to read English for hundreds of years. This used to be routine. It's as easy as A is for Apple.

Somehow we've got a new kind of "educator" and these people have a knack for non-education. They can take a bunch of ordinary kids and fix it so those kids never learn to read. You know what's really funny? These "educators" get paid for this.

How do you recognize these phonies? Easy. They'll tell you that every kid is different and you have to be willing to try a whole range of approaches. Phonics doesn't always work, they say, and isn't right for all kids. So here's their inane solution. Start teaching all these different approaches more or less simultaneously to all the kids, which guarantees confusion and more confusion.

Truth is, kids are essentially the same. The differences are minor. You need to teach all children the letters and sounds of the English language ASAP. There's a lot of consistency and logic. This is reassuring for children. B always stands for the same sound; and every B-word starts with that sound, e.g., beach, bingo, ball, brother, body, etc.

Our Education Establishment often wails, "English is weird and unpredictable." That's their excuse for promoting Sight-Words. "Oh, alas," they whine, "if only English were perfectly phonetic like Spanish and Italian."

Now let me tell you a really funny story. On the Internet you can find lists of Spanish Dolch words, which makes no sense in any logical universe. Furthermore, a group in Italy contacted me because the schools there were pushing Sight-Words into the classroom. To teach Italian? Again, this makes no sense unless we're dealing with con artists and fraudsters.

Just last week a teacher in Bosnia, of all places, informed me that they were teaching Serbian with Sight-Words (and literacy was falling). The teacher explained that Serbian has 30 letters that represent 30 sounds and is thus perfectly phonetic. Again, this development in Bosnia makes no sense unless you have (let's be frank) criminal educators intent on sabotaging literacy.

So you see, the bit about English not being perfectly phonetic is just a trick. They don't care what English is. All they care about is concocting a pretext for introducing methods that don't work. There are many, but Sight-Words are the preeminent example of a method that doesn't work.

The truth is, and it's not funny at all, it when you study reading theory and practice over the last 80 years, you see evil. You really do. You see teachers asking children to memorize the English language one graphic design at a time. It's not remotely possible except for that rare individual with a photographic memory. Memorizing even 500 Sight-Words is extremely difficult. But that's almost nothing against the vast multitude of the English language.

So here's the funny, as in weird, punchline. Children are being asked to put their elbows in their ears, to multiply five-digit numbers in their heads, to fly to the moon. It can't be done, and it's evil to pretend that it can be.

———

People in Favor of Dumb Schools,
Wave Your Arms in the Air
Like You Just Don't Care

Better still, make silly faces and tell knock-knock jokes.

Even better, put a bag over your eyes and flee to a dark room. Hide! Maybe then you won't notice the creeping dumbness crippling the country.

Maybe your conscience won't bother you as the schools dumb down additional tens of millions of children, making them ignorant and semiliterate.

Maybe you've already forgotten a time when people knew stuff: who Napoleon was, where Japan is on a globe, the number of stars on the US flag. Ah, those were brash and vibrant times. People could make references to common information and know they would be understood. *Yes, I'm telling you the truth!* People would say things like, "Nice play, Shakespeare." *Uh*, maybe I need to explain this. Shakespeare, you see, wrote plays. So when somebody did something goofy, people would say, "Nice play, Shakespeare." Well, you have to take my word for it. It's a clever remark. People would laugh. Really!

But never mind. All that is gone now. There is no common knowledge, no common culture. People know what they know and their friends know. But nobody knows what the people across town know. We're seeing the ultimate atomization

of a population. **Everyone is separate, everyone is alone, everyone knows close to zero. That's the secret, don't you see?**

Our elite educators have stolen the icing off the cake, the cherry off the banana split, the rainbow from the clouds. They are the dark angels of dumb, and they can't stand your learning any little thing. They have devised a medicine cabinet of pedagogical poisons, all designed to empty what is left of your brain. One of these gimmicks says that teachers should celebrate "prior knowledge." Well, little robots, that's the only kind you are going to have from now on—what you bring in the front door. Assuming they let you take it out. It's quite possible they won't approve of what you brought through the front door. In which case your mind will be strip-searched, and all that useless nonsense will be confiscated. In such cases, you won't have new knowledge, you won't have prior knowledge, you won't have no knowledge. You'll be perfect.

Well, maybe we have to applaud a job well done. It takes a kind of genius to create a population as ignorant as ours is today. Just look, we have 50 million functional illiterates, people who can't read beyond ordering a cheeseburger, filling the gas tank, or figuring out which streets to take to the mall. Schools are like Celebrity Jeopardy for Kids: foods that start with C; sounds a cat makes; distances that are not one mile. And those are the Honors Programs.

Doesn't it make you wonder, what kind of sickos are so in love with ignorance? Personally, I think facts are fun. I know that knowledge is power. There's my educational philosophy. With just those two slogans you could build world-class schools.

But our educators—what are their beliefs? Facts are wasted time; and knowledge is power they don't want you to have. How can they control you if you know anything? How can they dictate every detail of your life if you have a single opinion? **Thomas Jefferson said it so beautifully. You can't be both ignorant and free. So which is it, bub? You prefer ignorance? You like what the educators have done to you? Schools today are sort of like a lobotomy without the surgery. Didn't hurt at all, did it?**

Admit it, you don't know what a lobotomy is. You don't know who Thomas Jefferson is. I'll tell you, he was a president of the United States. Oh, sorry. You don't know what the United States is either.

They have taught you well. Our Education Establishment has turned education into a one-word oxymoron. Night descends. That barking dog you hear is us. "Nice Shakespeare, play." Makes just as much sense, doesn't it? "Play Shakespeare, nice." They all compute. That's the genius of our world now. Everything computes. Nothing computes. You're alive but dead. And why should that matter if you don't know? How could you know? You're in a dark room, with your eyes shut and a bag over your head, making sure you couldn't possibly know.

Because let me tell you, just start to think about it, even for a minute, then the pain will start. These images will stab through you, these vistas and visions, bright with energy and light, of you in a world full of information and knowledge and the excitement of dancing facts. Not all slack and stupid and dull like now.

No, this is you smart and getting smarter, learning stuff and knowing things, full of the most wonderfully interesting details, so that for the first time in your life, you feel alive. And you imagine yourself looking back with this huge swell of gratitude for all the dedicated schools you attended and the earnest well-educated teachers who awakened the fire in you. And you feel a joyful communion with these teachers and these schools and all the other students in them. And a friend does something silly and you say, "Nice play, Shakespeare." And everyone laughs.

8. GUILTY

**Are they clumsy or actually aiming for mediocrity?
Everything points to bad faith and malfeasance.**

If Public Schools Were a Business,
All of Top Management Would Be Fired

If it wasn't so tragic, it would be comical. In a society where everyone is immersed in language and surrounded by words, we somehow manage to have an illiteracy crisis.

Recent government tests show that two-thirds of the kids entering middle school are sub-literate. This country has 50 million borderline illiterates. Furthermore, SAT scores are falling. American students don't compete well against students from other countries, even though we spend vastly more per student than almost everybody else. Ordinary citizens know less and less general information. In short, public education is a disgraceful sham.

If public schools were a publicly traded corporation, it goes without saying that all the top people would be fired today. New management would be brought in. New policies would be tried until improvement was manifest to everyone. You know this is exactly what would happen in any practical, sensible part of the universe.

So the question must be: why has our Education Establishment been allowed to make a mess of things year after year? Did it win an election running on the incompetence platform? Can you attend a graduate school of education only if you sign your brain over to a cult?

Well, let's not indulge too much in the ridicule of the ridiculous. Let's focus on the main prize, which is to fix this mess.

The Education Establishment itself appears to be a self-perpetuating Rube Goldberg contraption. Gears squeak; that's too often all that happens. Virtually every elite educator since the time of John Dewey has been a denizen of the far-left. These socialists seem to think exactly alike; and they don't let in people who don't think alike. So we can't assume that the official experts are going to help. My conclusion is that they caused the problems; how can we expect them to turn around and fix the problems? So when we look at the Department of Education, National Education Association, and all the top people in the field somewhat ironically called "Education," we should know that we will simply get more of the same non-education.

Obviously we have to look to the larger world for leadership and salvation: prominent citizens, community and religious groups, private schools, conservative political groups, and particularly non-profit organizations. Many of the big-name non-profit organizations in business, politics, military, and other fields are officially devoted to education reform. (Often, these groups solicit funds for that exact purpose. But education stays the same or gets worse. Isn't that intriguing? I've called up some of these organizations to ask: are you really doing all you can? Contributors should ask the same thing.)

In all cases, we need to move to a higher level of seriousness. The Education Establishment, intent on its ideological goals, has dumbed down not just the schools but almost every discussion about schools. We're trying to discuss the architecture for a new building even as we are dog-paddling around in a swamp. First, let's drain the swamp. Then we need a lot more people with what Hemingway called "a good bullshit detector." Virtually everything the official educators come up with is either trivial, a distraction, or outright BS. Let's call it what it is as a simple first step toward reform.

Seriously, folks, you simply cannot create 50 million more or less illiterate people without some serious stupidity or you are trying very hard. Isn't that a fair statement? It's not as though young kids are living in the jungle and never see a printed word. No, we are all surrounded by language from the time we open our eyes. TV ads. Packaging. Magazines. Billboards. Menus. It's almost inconceivable that our public schools can actually *prevent* children from learning to read—that's how I would put it—but prevent reading is exactly what they do. Ditto so much else that used to be taught in public schools.

Quick, find some top-level educrats and say: you are fired!

The Truth About Education??? You Can't Handle the Truth.

Our Education Establishment, in plain sight, is doing a terrible job. Who, we should ask, is in charge of this train wreck, and what motivates them?

First, let's add up the evidence. The one million dyslexics. The poor performance against international competition, despite our huge budgets. The ignorance of average Americans about basic geographical, historical, and scientific information. SAT scores slide; kids cannot multiply and divide; students reach college not knowing what six times seven is. About 65% of the children in fourth and eighth grades are reading at a level below "proficient," that is, they are in some sense illiterate.

That's a dismal record. In any other field, the people in charge would be fired, disqualified, disbarred, drummed out of office, or indicted.

In 1953, Professor Arthur Bestor wrote a book called *Educational Wastelands—the Retreat From Learning in Our Public Schools*. Our education bosses have been doing a lousy job for more than 60 years— that's well chronicled. Explaining why they persist in doing a bad job is the hard part.

You can play all the evidence back and forth in your mind for a year; I predict you will finally come down to four possible explanations. All unpleasant to contemplate. But let's try.

First, these people are less than competent. Education is not a field known for recruiting brainiacs, not since 1950. Now it seems to be an intellectual backwater. The main recurrent image is a large school of slow fish drifting from fad to fad.

Second, the elite educators are lost in cloud-cuckoo land. That is, they rarely meet a theory, however silly, that they don't fall in love with. So they can promote counterproductive ideas without even realizing how bad the ideas are.

Third, we are always told to follow the money. In this case it's important to note that ordinary minds can make an excellent living in education. They have titles, credentials, prestige. All they need do is agree with their superiors.

Fourth, they are subversives deliberately trying to undermine our society. Recall that in the 1930s, John Dewey and his progressive educators announced that public schools must be transformed, so the country could be transformed. That's code for creating a socialist country, no matter how few people want it.

Which of the four explanations is best? Well, humans are usually driven by a messy mix of motives. When we are talking about the lower and middle levels of the Education Establishment, I can imagine those people being propelled by all four motivations.

However, as we consider the top level of the Education Establishment, the smartest and most powerful people, don't we have to assume much greater awareness? There is so much obvious decay, so much intellectual decline, so many dreadful statistics. Surely, the top-tier people have to know exactly what they're doing and why.

One distinctive thing about the field of education is that the elite people rarely confess or write tell-all memoirs. Further, the media don't do much investigative journalism. You almost never see, in a newspaper, any in-depth analysis explaining educational failure. So we have to use our intuition and solve this mystery as best we can.

I tend to suspect the top people can't be driven primarily by incompetence, love of theory, or money. Doesn't there have to be ideological commitment? Remember, millions of kids are being damaged, year after year, decade after decade. This is no job for weekend warriors. You have to be a hardcore "change agent."

Recall that these elite educators embraced Whole Word in 1931; in 1955, Flesch explained why it didn't work. But here we are 60 years later and the schools are still churning out millions of citizens who can't read. Dwell on that. These education commissars decided to keep pushing a clunker no matter what. How many people have that kind of will and discipline?

So I'm seeing, at least at the pinnacle, a small group of dedicated fanatics. Perhaps, as we look at the entire field of education, there are only five or ten people who actually know what is going on and make the big decisions. Maybe at the top there is only one guy who really knows.

Maybe the question we should be asking about the Education Establishment is precisely this: who is the person actually pulling the strings? Who is Jabba the Hutt?

He, as you may remember from Star Wars, is an intergalactic crime lord and all-around bad boy. of course, that's just my personal image of a guy who could create millions of functional illiterates.

Now, many foolish state legislators accepted Obama's bribes to sign on to Common Core Curriculum. All this means is that Jabba the Hutt and his crew will have more power than ever, if that's possible.

Each of these top professors has mentored one or two dozen Ph.D. candidates. I imagine the top guys putting the word out to their loyal lieutenants, and they to theirs. The word could be passed down through a phone tree in an hour. Message: support Plan X. And the next thing you know, Plan X flows out into all the schools. Because Jabba the Hutt said so.

So I suspect serious scheming at the top, perhaps overseen by a godfather or two. Malfeasance and conspiracy are the perennial themes. Otherwise, the relentless tide of bad stats that we see could never have been achieved.

Is this too harsh a vision? Well, when people are incompetent for so long, it's altogether fitting and proper to harbor dark thoughts about them.

Here's more bad news. Even as the public is generally cowed and confused, the groups and forces that should be protecting the society are passive. Remarkably, business and the military now, like the media and academia before them, don't seem to try very hard. A phenomenon that strikes me as more and more alarming.

What is the way out? We shouldn't listen to the people presiding over our educational decline. Let's oppose them or at the least ignore them.

Meanwhile, let's learn from what the best in the field do. Every city has three reservoirs of educational knowledge: people in charge of the good private schools; managers of the best parochial schools; and homeschooling parents (these people have to teach all day; you know they don't waste time on methods that don't work).

So my goal here is to drive a wedge between ordinary citizens, and the ideologues who are mismanaging public education. Ignore the latter. Copy only what the best schools do.

Let's create public schools that will take each child as far as each one can go. Skip the indoctrination. Stop the busy-work. Put the education back in education. It'll be a beautiful thing.

———

Education: A Walk on the Wild Side

Feeling brave? Got a cast-iron stomach? Not offended by decadence? Well, come with me and we'll go for a stroll in the dangerous part of town, where society's bad boys hang out. Yes, I'm talking about Education.

One metaphor works best for this whole disturbing field, and that's CSI. Imagine a really big crime scene, chaotic and messy, filled with walking wounded, people who can't read or count, their brains empty, their thoughts incoherent.

What happened here? We need to figure out whodunit and why? A wife stages the death of her husband for the insurance; that's an easy one. **Public education, the crime scene we are entering, has hundreds of major suspects, their deeds spread over many decades, the evidence murky, mostly hidden from view. All we know for dead certain is that millions of Americans have been victims of a crime wave.**

In 1955 Rudolf Flesch wrote his bestseller titled *Why Johnny Can't Read.* To a large degree, Flesch triggered the reading wars and homeschooling. Good reading is so basic, so necessary for even the most elementary education. And it's so easy to test; you put a newspaper in front of a child and say, read this. Then you know everything, possibly much more than you want to know. One of the most common scenes in America since 1935 is the illiteracy epiphany. *Oh my God, our kid can't read! Is he brain-damaged?*

Flesch explained the whole thing. Nothing complicated. The public schools had stopped using phonics (kids learn the alphabet and the sounds that the letters stand for). Public school officials were forcing children to memorize words as graphic designs, as we memorize the Nike logo, currency symbols, or UN flags. Disciplined children with exceptional memories can possibly read with sight-words. Ordinary kids are destroyed. By fourth grade they might learn only a few hundred sight-words. But not with automaticity. Mostly, such kids just fumble and guess.

All right, so the top educators (i.e., professors of education and superintendents) really goofed. They launched an untested, unproven method, first called Look-say (and many other aliases). At the time, you might have concluded all this was an innocent mistake. They meant well. But after Flesch explained the misadventure in 150 lucid pages and everyone knew the score, an odd thing happened. The Education Establishment went to the mattresses for Whole Word. According to them, Flesch was a crazed malcontent. **Our elite educators (at Harvard's Graduate School of Education and such places) were going to make kids learn to read sight-words or die trying. Not the educators. It was the kids who would die trying.**

The main method for teaching children to read in the United States from 1932 until quite recently has been Sight-Words. Even now, many educators pretend to embrace phonics, but children in the first few grades are forced to memorize so-called Dolch words. This process guarantees that children are slowed down and confused. Does all this seem quaint and academic to you? Quite the opposite. It's raw and ruthless.

This country has at least 50 million semi-literate citizens. These people should be reading books for fun. They can't do this; and what makes it so poignant is that they have no idea what was done to them or how to escape from the hit. Meanwhile, the experts who did the dirty work give each other awards, grants, professorships, and million-dollar publishing contracts. Crime does pay.

Some might call the Education Establishment a RICO enterprise. For ideological reasons, they decided they didn't want children to be individualistic or competitive. They wanted to make them all more or less the same. Our Education Establishment bought into leveling; and that meant a furtive undercutting of achievement, knowledge, and even reading. Kids who know too much will advance beyond the other kids and feel superior. You might think that reading is always a good thing; these progressive educators did not agree with you. A book published in 1958 mentions: *"Public school administrators have gone so far as to assert that they look hopefully for the day when learning to read will not be considered more important than learning to sew or skate."*

I told you, this is a bad part of town. Quacks and swindlers lurk everywhere. Ah, look, there is New Math, which did for arithmetic what Look-say did for reading. The boys in the back room must have been proud. But this gimmick, which flourished for a few years around 1964, was so obviously unworkable (and vicious), that the whole country booed it off the stage. Kids couldn't learn. Parents hated it. Teachers were bewildered. New Math vanished so quickly it's easy to miss the main element of this story. Some of the smartest people in education (probably all with PhD's) spent 15 years preparing this con. They went too far. Point is, they tried. Museums should be built to New Math. It serves to remind everyone that the Education Establishment has a predilection for shady products that damage children.

New Math morphed some years later into Reform Math. Kids couldn't learn. Parents hated it. Teachers were bewildered. See a pattern?

There, in the shadows, more bad actors: Open Classroom, Life Adjustment, Self-Esteem, Multiculturalism, Relevance, No Memorization, Bilingual Education, the list goes on and on. Arguably, every method the top educators really love invariably turns out to be a Ponzi scheme.

The one thing these people are good at is marketing. Bad ideas with sweet-sounding names are forced into every classroom. Appreciate the genius in all these slick phrases: Constructivism, Cooperative Learning, Discovery Method, Whole Language, 21st-Century Skills, Common Core Standards, and many more. We don't know what they mean but they sure do sound good.

In a short space, I can't explain the inner machinery that renders each idea destructive. The important fact is that these gimmicks don't work very well (and are routinely replaced by other fads) but they are pushed for a time with brutal abandon. In all other parts of life, if bosses come up with stuff that doesn't work, they go out of business, they are fired, or voted out of office. But in education they are promoted. This is a gang or cult (more like a religion than most people realize). You can't be successful unless you embrace the creed that your mentors embraced. And in this way education is locked in dumb.

The media don't explain the cartel's long and reckless history, and its far-left DNA. Typically, the explanations we see are shallow; and you may be left wondering why we have so many problems. So let's cut to the chase. The cheap and easy way to improve education is simply to root out the dishonest ideas that the top educators have pushed for the past century.

Almost every article written on education, for many years, mentions in passing that two-thirds of fourth graders can't read at grade level. Two-thirds! So that's this year's batch of functional illiterates that the schools are churning out. There's no excuse. Really think about it, and you'll be angry. Good, now we can start taking back the neighborhood.

Church of Knowledge vs Church of Indoctrination

Many people, confronting the mediocrity and malaise of the public schools, are dumbfounded. Why have things gotten so bad? As long ago as 1983, a government report said that our schools seem to have been designed by a hostile foreign power. More recently, in 2007, Bill Gates led a commission which concluded that the public schools are a threat to our country's future.

How do we explain all this? Here is the easiest way.

For thousands of years people started schools for only one reason. They knew a lot of information; and they believed this information was vital to young people. The purpose of education, obviously, was to transmit knowledge to the next generation. All educators, since the beginning of history, were worshippers in the Church of Knowledge.

It's not like that anymore. Virtually everyone in the top levels of education has long ago left that church. They may not comprehend its beliefs at all. They have joined a different church with a different creed.

Since the time of John Dewey, top educators became members of the Church of Indoctrination. Everything they do during the school day is focused on turning out a child socialized in a certain way, not an educated child. These educators see the school as a socialist training ground, a place where high-minded social engineers (them) can create a wonderful new kind of humans who will build a brave new world. (Note that the social engineers themselves will rule this world—certainly a conflict of interest.)

So the crux of our problem is simple. These top educators are not in the education business anymore, not as most of us understand that phrase. We foolishly suppose that they are trying to do something they are not trying to do. They will provide head fakes and sophistries to keep us fooled. But they know what their priorities are: collectivist indoctrination. Knowledge, if it's considered at all, is viewed as a nuisance, like a kid having to brush his teeth.

Perhaps the thing that no one anticipated is that knowledge would so often appear to be directly in the way of the social schemes. So, diminishing knowledge a little did not turn out to be workable. Getting rid of as much knowledge as possible often seemed more helpful to the cause. Consider a few examples:

Math and science generally are precise and insist on objective truth. But the socialist educators were pushing theories that can't necessarily be proven. Why encourage children to become able to discuss these things? Indeed, why teach children to think for themselves at all?

Furthermore, math and science tend to be easier for boys. Well, in this collectivist world, you don't want one group of kids moving ahead of another group of kids. So there's a very good reason for undercutting math and science, which the educators tried to do in Reform Math (most memorably in the curriculum called Mathland).

Consider foreign languages. Words must be spelled a certain way and pronounced a certain way–these are approaches that modern schools downplayed in the teaching of English. Indeed many children were never taught to read and pronounce English words phonetically. Imagine the conflicts that would've arisen if French et al were taught in the early years. So what happened? Almost across the board, public schools got rid of foreign languages in the first six grades, even though all experts said this was the best time to teach a foreign language!

What about History? Do we want to make heroes of patriotic Americans? Rich capitalists? Tycoons, inventors and famous generals? No, we do not. We want the children to think of everybody as more or less the same. Nobody is supposed to try to move ahead of other people. This creates social friction. Socialist thinkers don't want any of those things, so History is really a hindrance. Not to mention, most of the participants over the last several thousand years were males. Talking about famous males is another no-no. Not to mention a lot of the most interesting events occurred in wars. That's another no-no if you're trying to encourage pacifistic cooperation.

What about Geography? Why can't we teach that? Well, if Americans can look at how other people live around the world, American kids might start feeling very proud about themselves and their country. Obviously we can't have that!

All our problems become really simple if you put yourself in the place of the bishops in the Church of Indoctrination. Imagine that your goal is social engineering. Then every policy these people preferred will seem completely logical to you. You would find yourself doing precisely the same thing. You would downplay and devalue everything that was traditionally done in the schools, i.e., teaching knowledge. Meanwhile, you would focus all your resources on molding and shaping little children to be whatever it is you think they should be. Form a vision in your mind of how you think children should be. Then imagine you set up a school to make exactly that happen, and only that. Further imagine that your idea of what children should be is at variance with what the society wants or cares about. Well, you will be in a long-running campaign, a war really, against the parents, the local customs and culture, against all the things done over the centuries by concerned parents and genuine schools. Thus the Education Wars.

To make this thought experiment complete, you have to suppose that you have become really obsessed and even ruthless on the subject of social engineering. You've gone so completely over to collectivist thinking that the very idea of grades strikes you as repulsive. The thought of some children being given Honors or one child being picked as valedictorian makes you want to vomit. Now you'll start to feel the need for ever more indoctrination.

As long as such extremists are in charge, we will have a dumbed-down curriculum and mediocre schools. They don't even seem to be very good as indoctrination centers. Look at all the crime, the bullying, the drugs, the dropping out, the giving up. So whatever kind of child our so-called educators are trying to create, they are not doing a very good job. Meanwhile, they're very much succeeding in destroying the concept of the educated citizen as we used to understand that phrase.

So I keep coming back to the same dire conclusion. We have to replace these so-called experts. Many people may remember Senator Patrick Moynihan and his famous comment that he would prefer to be ruled by 400 people out of the phone book than by the faculty at Harvard. That is such a brilliant insight. If our schools were run by any 400 people in the phone book (let's qualify that by saying they should have some college), I would feel comfortable saying the schools would be much better. Presumably these people will be trying to make the schools work, as opposed to not work. These 400 would for the most part be lifelong members of the Church of Knowledge. Improvement would ensue automatically.

———

Explaining the Cynicism of Our Top Educators

Probably the most famous example of world-class cynicism is the wrought-metal sign above the gate into Auschwitz. Three German words: ARBEIT MACHT FREI (usually translated "work makes you free").

The sign undoubtedly provided hope to many prisoners. (If we work hard, we will be released!) But these prisoners, no matter how hard they worked, were en route to a tragic fate. There was no hope; the sign was a lie.

Of course, we are not surprised if a Nazi prison turns out to be dishonest and murderous. But what about our public schools? Surely, they would not stoop to cynicism and insincerity. I started thinking about this because the schools do make an offer that is conceptually parallel (albeit, a world apart) to the one above the gate.

The schools say: sit in our classrooms, endure the boredom, do your lessons, read books you may not enjoy, learn things you don't want to know... and in return for all this work, you will be made free. Free to pursue a career, free to advance socially and financially, free to follow your dreams.

Probably every school since the beginning of history offered students some version of this trade-off. Study hard and thereby move ahead. But this proposal was especially crucial—and welcomed—in a dynamic, fluid society like the United States circa 1900. Immigrants came from all over the world to pursue the American Dream. Their children went to the public schools for the same reason.

And then something happened. Dewey's so-called Progressives (a/k/a socialists and collectivists) commandeered the training of teachers and gained control over the daily activities inside tens of thousands of schools. The focus shifted to social engineering. All of this was done in stealth. Cynicism loomed.

Socialists were not concerned with people moving ahead. Socialists were fixated on convincing people that they would be better off in a socialist society. When people were slow to accept this claim, socialists resorted to more aggressive measures: they filled the curricula in every grade with propaganda and discarded ever more academic content.

As we moved into mid-20th century, the Education Establishment was engaged in an increasingly cynical campaign. They said to the incoming students: we want to educate you. In fact, the public schools had veered off into an obsession with non-education (this being probably the best term for what happened to public education in this country during the last hundred years: non-education was labeled as education).

There was an endless emphasis on fancy new reasons for doing things in fancy new ways. But fundamentally all of this was bait-and-switch. Education, as most parents understand that term, was promised. However, what was actually delivered was an inferior, watered-down education that is more accurately called indoctrination.

The showpiece for this bait-and-switch is Whole Word. Flesch explained in 1955 why it was a hoax; I'm satisfied he was right. Virtually no one learns to read English by memorizing tens of thousands of graphic designs. But the Education Establishment started pushing this thing in 1931 and still has not stopped.

Consider the cynicism. You tell children: do what we say and you will learn to read. No, they will become illiterate, dyslexic and learning-disabled. It's such a horrible, obvious lie that many of the older teachers refused to follow this gimmick and secretly taught phonics when the doors were closed. Other teachers had to be threatened. New waves of teachers needed to be indoctrinated in graduate school. Some of the cleverest sophists who ever lived helped create the indoctrination for Whole Word.

Now replicate this story dozens of times, in all subjects: lame, counterproductive methods are foisted on the public with the help of slick misinformation. (That sentence can serve as a Micro-History of American Public Education.)

The point is, ever since roughly 1920, our Education Establishment has not been primarily interested in setting people "free." These so-called educators are passionately concerned with making people socialists. It's the lying about it that I want to point out now: the promising of one thing while cynically delivering something else.

The people running Auschwitz knew what they were doing, knew that the metal sign was endlessly cynical. I have to suspect that the people now in control of the schools, professors of education and so forth, know precisely what they are doing.

The problem with becoming a slave to ideology is that you no longer find it unacceptable or even strange that you want to turn everyone else into a slave.

———

Education as the Road to Serfdom

The Latin root of educate is to "lead out from," as Moses led the Jews out from Egypt. The original concept was that children are living in ignorance, and we would naturally want to lead them from that world into a better world. A world where they know more and have more options.

Freedom is central to this original concept. As you become educated—that is, as you learn more—you move from less freedom to more freedom. When George Washington, Benjamin Franklin and the other founders talked about public education, they were clearly thinking of schools that would liberate children.

So, education leads us away from ignorance, and into a promised land of greater knowledge and more freedom. Isn't that a fair statement of how it's supposed to work?

Generally speaking, I suspect most people want education to work precisely like this. In fact, all too often it doesn't.

Surprisingly, perversely, public education in the USA does not venerate knowledge, and is not sufficiently concerned with creating freedom. This is our great national tragedy.

Around a century ago, a curious thing happened. The field of education ended up betraying its original intentions. This is a tangled story best summarized by noting that two storm fronts swept across the American landscape.

Henry Ford and the industrialists wanted docile, cooperative workers who would show up on time, follow instructions and not cause trouble. Control was the key concept. **Freedom was hardly part of this picture.**

Simultaneously, our "progressives"—socialists in everything but name—wanted docile, cooperative citizens who would follow instructions and not cause trouble. These progressives moved massively into the field of education, with the intent of using the public schools to create children who would grow up to be socialists. Control and manipulation were constant preoccupations. **Freedom was hardly part of this picture.**

Across the landscape, wherever you might look, the new fields of Sociology, Psychology and Education were allies in a war for control of the rambunctious American population. John Dewey, the father of American education, merely voiced what all these new elites believed: Americans were too individualistic and self-determined. This had to be stopped. John Dewey and his friends were eager to accept the job. Individuality was for these people a dirty word.

As several decades passed, our industrialists became more threatened by what was going on in Europe and Russia than what was going on here politically. Furthermore, jobs increasingly needed smart workers. So this part of the story tended to soften.

However, all the machinations on the socialist side hardened into dogma. I think it's fair to say that by 1950 the field of education was more a cult than anything else. Nobody questioned the premises embraced at Columbia's Teachers College. The endless plotting and scheming in the name of control was all part of a day's work. In a double whammy, many of these so-called educators were doubtless motivated by wanting to help Russia win the Cold War.

When you look at the minimalist academic curricula proposed by the professors circa 1950, you're struck by how completely these people had turned away from knowledge. They said they wanted to teach children how to find a job, fill out forms, dress for success, ride the subway, decorate a house, and drive a car. Some leading educators even spoke up against the importance of literacy. Reading wasn't such a big deal, after all. The people pushing this dumbing-down had a clear sense of purpose: they wanted to make little socialists. You can't say this too often. The classroom was a laboratory for making little socialists. Everything else was secondary. Knowledge and freedom were secondary.

Over the last century, education as higher consciousness lost a duel with education as a new kind of consciousness. Schools today are full of theories and methods designed to limit consciousness. At last, that's my cynical conclusion.

For me, the most startling thing about the public schools is that most Americans persist in hoping, praying, assuming that the Education Establishment actually means well, despite a track record which shows it doesn't mean well. The word "conspiracy" is unpleasant for many people; and yet I don't see how you can discuss John Dewey and his successors without understanding that every time they talked to each other, they were conspiring to control what children learned and what they became.

Once you factor in all of this, you won't be so surprised that we have 50,000,000 functional illiterates, that many college kids don't know what 5 times 8 is, or that I received a press release declaring: "The Council on Foreign Relations' task force sounds the alarm that America's education crisis is fast becoming a national security threat. Embarrassingly, American students are far worse off than other developed countries, despite the U.S. outspending all developed nations on K-12 education."

To save ourselves, we have to give up education as social engineering (that is, a tool for control), and return to a respect for knowledge and a love of freedom. Unfortunately, I'm afraid our Education Establishment will fight such proposals with all their strength.

———

Biggest Bullies in the Public Schools: The Education Establishment

We hear a lot about bullying as if it's as common as cheering at a football game.

But who is really the Big Bully in our public schools? Who is throwing their weight around all the time?

More specifically, who is insisting on the use of bad methods that never seem to work better this year than 10 years ago? Who is making lame excuses for poor performance so that nothing seems to get better? Who fills the air with propaganda and sophistry so that no one can think clearly about the issues facing us?

Consider Whole Word. Rudolf Flesch exposed this hoax 60 years ago but it's embedded in our public schools. Consider Reform Math which parents have been complaining about for 30 years but it's still confounding students in our public schools. Consider Constructivism, which forbids teachers from teaching. Wouldn't everyone predict that less is going to be taught? Of course, but this gimmick is more and more enshrined in public schools.

What kind of bullies would demand that inferior methods be used? "Let them eat cake" seems to be the Education Establishment's entire plan.

Now we have the imposition of Common Core Standards, which wants to mandate what happens in every classroom in the country. As a frustrated teacher in Delaware noted: "I call it Common Bore. The idea is that there is no more autonomy in lesson plans and instruction. We have 90 minutes per week of PLC's (Professional Learning Communities) meetings that are designed to encourage us to present information uniformly to our students. That is not realistic when teachers are just as much individuals and have our own 'styles', as are the students we teach. For these reasons, I'm disgusted. I don't want to teach anymore."

Another teacher complained on the Internet: "I just read a post in a Charter School discussion group that basically said that CCS requires constructivist education, and that any teacher who didn't like it should be forced out of the profession or leave!"

Common Core Standards sounds more like a control freak's fantasy than a serious attempt to improve education.

This punitive pattern has been evident for most of the past century, as noted in Siegfried Engelmann's seminal book "War Against The Schools's Academic Child Abuse." Note that phrase: "academic child abuse." That is what bullies naturally do.

The main feature of Common Core is that the federal government gains power to enforce its favorite clunkers. Looking at dozens of methods across dozens of years, we can see that the essential trick is to find slow, inefficient ways to teach everything. Arguably, that is child abuse. Children become discouraged and exhausted. They give up trying to do things that they can easily do, and this includes fundamental things such as reading and arithmetic. All that students are sure of is that they learn to hate reading and arithmetic.

The second big gimmick is to introduce so many secondary details that the class is distracted and disorganized. Teachers must learn about a student's prior experiences and their learning styles. Straight-ahead, gung-ho teaching is disparaged.

So the essence of this bullying is to confine children to a small world. They never know what wonderful things education can accomplish and how much fun it can be.

Children cannot analyze the methods used and explain why they fail. It's the administrators who should stand back and look at what's done to kids. They can remember their own education. They can contact private schools and see how subjects are taught there. They can call a friend in another city and ask what's going on in those schools.

There is no excuse for people in a public school to do a bad job. But they go right on doing it. All this bad pedagogy seems to be aimed at what, in the Vietnam era, was called "pacification." The goal seems to be to freeze students at a mediocre level.

In many schools, everybody is running, running, running but somehow everyone ends up in the same spot. Socialist educators are interested in what they call social justice, which tends to mean uniformity. To get that, you need to do some serious dumbing down.

Suppose you draft people into the military and give them undemanding, incoherent training. If sent off to war, most will be quickly killed because they lack basic skills.

What kind of preparation is that? Many students are not getting proper instruction for life because the bullies in charge won't let them have it.

Made Dumb In USA

This country has a bizarre and unprecedented problem. "The longer American children are in school, the worse they perform compared to their international peers," according to McKinsey and Company, management consultants.

Columnists at the New York Times have realized that the education crisis is grave. Tom Friedman said we're falling off a cliff. Paul Krugman noticed our dilemma but wants to blame it on a lack of money, which is nonsense. Education budgets are massive. Here's a better theory: the people in charge are evidently not all that interested in excellence. Nicholas Kristof pointed out that "Democrats have... stood by as generations of disadvantaged children had been cemented into an underclass by third-rate schools." Thank you, Mr. Kristof.

My guess is that the Education Establishment (i.e., the people in charge of creating third-rate schools) are real proud. I'm not

being ironic. Dumbing-down is, I conclude, their philosophy and their goal.

Are you wondering why? Simple. These guys, from John Dewey onward, were Socialists, obsessed with making children fit into a new socialist paradigm. Academic success was not essential; it might even be an obstacle to the collectivist plans these people had for us.

What about how? Again, simple. Favor the non-academic and the anti-academic. Let's say you have two pedagogical methods. Option A works better than Z. Drum roll, please. Agonize but, in the end, select Z. Concoct some good marketing prose to sell this pathetic thing. But use what does not work.

So far as I can tell, every method and approach embraced by the Education Establishment, for the past 100 years, ends up somewhere between dumb and dumber. (One might ask: are these people incompetent or purposeful? It's not likely that anybody can be that incompetent, so I'm seeing intent.)

In any event, our educators created schools so dysfunctional that they would make students worse with each passing year, as Mckinsey and Company stated.

To recap the reason: all the main methods (and there are dozens) used in the public schools turn out to be surprisingly counter-productive. Here's a quick look at some of the worst offenders:

Whole Word has the peculiar property of not teaching children to read. 50,000,000 functional illiterates is a lot of dumbing-down.

Reform Math has the peculiar property of making sure that children can't do basic arithmetic, even by college.

Constructivism (which is popular in many different subjects) has the peculiar property of making sure that children learn less than they did the year before. (Constructivism requires that children invent their own new knowledge, which takes a lot of extra time.)

Cooperative Learning has the peculiar property of making kids less independent and less able to think for themselves. This technique is helpful if you're trying to create a herd mentality.

Outcomes-Based Education has the peculiar property of directing students toward very trivial goals (i.e., outcomes), such as discussing a movie or preparing a scrapbook.

One of the more popular methods is called **Self-Esteem.** Doesn't it sound good? In fact, this thing dismantles education in several different ways. First of all, it requires praising children who do a bad job. Children become accustomed to gold stars and compliments even if they haven't cracked a book. Why should they bother with books? But Self-Esteem is more insidious than so far suggested. Suppose you want your class to know the 10 states nearest to where they live. Some students won't get the whole list; they will feel badly about themselves. What to do? Cut the list to six. But next year, some children may not recall the shorter list. So the list will be cut to four. Then the teachers will decide that this is too demanding and "students can look it up." So you see that Self-Esteem undercuts from every direction until there is nothing left standing.

In 1983 a huge government commission concluded that our public schools are so bad they may as well have been designed by a hostile foreign power. That's the incompetence that Friedman and colleagues were talking about; but they just can't come out and say the truth. Namely, people like themselves—other liberals—were the culprits in charge. But how do they admit this after so much damage has piled up?

Meanwhile, the Business Roundtable reports that managers are struggling to find trained workers. Businesses are "wrestling with an undertrained workforce: Half see a sizable gap between their needs and employees' skills."

Well, I can just imagine that our Education Establishment is tickled pink.

What do we do? Fire from the top. That's what we would do in any other area of human activity. Colossal failure year after year? Fire the bosses. Second, dismantle the anti-intellectual infrastructure that is evident everywhere throughout the school system. Get rid of a mentality that dotes on social engineering, and replace it with a mindset that glorifies intellectual engineering.

More than anything else, however, we simply need to tell the truth. Schools don't get so bad unless somebody wants them that way. The USA is afflicted with an Education Establishment that is anti-education.

9. MOVERS AND SHAKERS

Why are they so passive, so indifferent? We need our big shots to move and shake more than they do.

Education: Let Down by Our Leaders

Many Americans feel abandoned, first, by the people officially in charge of education: National Education Association, Department of Are you a call why Education, National Council of Teachers of Math, National Council of Teachers of English, the Common Core Consortium, and another 25 groups with pretentious names and sly agendas. These groups have plotted, many suspect, to dumb down our public schools.

If learning is taking place, elite educators have a knack for formulating new policies and practices that end up neutralizing those occasional bits of good news. For parents, it's a Kafka thing. They're in an endless labyrinth, and never find release.

Not just the people officially in charge of education have let us down. All those who should be protecting us from these strange invaders have faded away. Where are the media of all kinds, where are the elite universities, where is the Chamber of Commerce? Where's the business community, where is the old money while they let the public schools subside into mediocrity? Where are the community leaders who should be fighting the progressive educators at every point? Why have the good guys abdicated?

Rudolf Flesch explained why Whole Word couldn't work in 1955. But Whole Word remains entrenched in the elementary grades, perhaps the longest running hoax in American history. **Why did the people at the top of the society allow such a travesty?**

Overload—that's how the Education Establishment keeps everyone tired and befuddled. They've got a dozen main methods that don't work as promised. What better way to keep people from noticing the defects then to propose a barrage of bad new methods on top of bad old methods? Common Core contains provisions for assessing what is called "text complexity," the goal being to make sure kids aren't reading anything too easy. Similarly, there's a technique that recommends "close reading" of difficult texts As many kids can hardly read at all, these techniques are spurious. They distract from the real goal, that kids learn to read fast and for pleasure.

The Education Establishment does not seem to respect parents, their beliefs, their allegiances. If anything, the Education Establishment seems to prefer squashing those things. There is a war waged by left-wing progressives, people who know they have all the answers. On the other side are parents, communities, families, religions, everything that might be called traditional. The progressives want to stifle the traditional. The Education Establishment is perhaps best understood as an occupying force like the Germans in France in 1942. We need more Resistance.

Academics have noted: "Detecting deception is difficult because there are no known completely reliable indicators of deception. Deception, however, places a significant cognitive load on the deceiver. He or she must recall previous statements so that his or her story remains consistent and believable."

This insight perhaps explains one of the most striking features of American education. Every possible theory and claim, no matter how discredited, is kept in play. How can anyone sort them out? We don't see any comparative testing; we see nothing empirical in the whole field. There is simply a cacophony of claims and arguments—a good setting for deception.

QED: we need less of almost everything the Education Establishment promotes.

Conversely, we need more homeschooling and private schools, more charter schools, more choice, more parallel education on the Internet. What we need more than anything is leadership. The leaders who should be protecting us and guiding us have abandoned the field. We have been let down by our leaders. It's as if the elders are on tranquilizers.

Many people are waiting for them to wake up. Perhaps it's better not to wait. In every community, there are people who had the blessing of good education, and their children received a good education. These people understand the value of a good education, and know what it looks like. They should step forward and explain to their neighbors what is going on. Provide the leadership our leaders are no longer giving.

———

Listen to Me, You Rich Successful People in Your Mansions

I know, I know, you don't want to think about all the bad public schools out there. Nothing to do with you, right?? Wrong. The effects are oozing through the society. You are in danger.

Want safety? Here are three threats we have to overcome:

1) THE EDUCATION ESTABLISHMENT CAN'T BE TRUSTED. Almost a century ago, they took a wrong turn, and went down a road marked SOCIAL ENGINEERING. The problem for everybody else is that these ideologues hope to wreck the society we've got, so they can build the collectivized world they dream about.

They justify the planned transformation with this bit of fluff from John Dewey: "Not knowledge or information, but self-realization, is the goal." What a quack. After all, it's new knowledge that typically leads students to self-realization. The Left wants to use schools to turn kids into compliant comrades; this truth can't be told, so a lot that goes on in our schools is disingenuous. Educators prattle endlessly about "education," but their true passion is making sure that very little of it, in the ordinary sense, occurs.

2) BIG MEDIA AND ELITE UNIVERSITIES ARE PART of THE PROBLEM. The media seem to think they should take orders from the NEA, etc. I see this pattern unfolding in my town, where the local paper will run 50 articles about one of its favorite liberal issues, but not one line about why a quarter of the kids don't learn to read, or drop out of school.

Professors at the best universities should have jumped into the Education Wars, the Math Wars, the Reading Wars. But I can't discover a single professor at my Ivy League school who stepped forward to support Rudolf Flesch or to decry the decline of the public schools.

We have to be disappointed that so many professors and journalists allowed themselves to be co-opted by the Education Establishment.

Bottom line, we can't expect help from the people who SHOULD be saving us.

3) WORSE STILL, MOST BIG SHOTS DON'T CARE. Talk to doctors, lawyers, bankers, brokers, executives, psychiatrists, movers and shakers of all kinds. Try to find one who knows anything about education or cares. They went to a good school years ago. Their kids went to private schools. Public schools are for them like a bad neighborhood on the other side of town; there's no reason for them to think about it.

———

Listen to me, you rich, successful people. A bad part of town will stay put, but the neighborhood called bad education is now oozing along your street. It's seeping through the walls of your house, and into your living room. You might not escape. Tens of millions of people who can't count, can't read, can't do a job correctly, don't know enough to care about voting—this uneducated horde will hurt every part of your life. What stake do they have in sustaining a civilization they don't understand and know little about?

So what is the answer to this hopeless situation? Here it is: all practical, successful people—in order to save their own skins—have to be much more involved.

The Education Establishment has a genius for finding the counter-intuitive, likely-to-fail approach. Almost everything is backwards. Business executives, forced to spend a day in a public school, might have nervous breakdowns. But you know what the even goofier problem is? A bunch of business leaders, eager to make improvements, would hire consultants from some place like Harvard's Graduate School of Education! The very people who created all the problems. That's how cowed and bamboozled everyone is.

No, the practical, successful people must stick to their MBA guns. Be businesslike. Ignore the faux-experts. Do what works, for a change.

I'd argue that the biggest hoax of the last 100 years is Whole Word. (It's the reason we have so many functional illiterates.) So a good first step for every concerned citizen is to understand WHY Sight-Words don't work. When you personally understand the deception, you'll be angry. Maybe then you'll get busy and get bold. We need you.

Then find out why New Math and Reform Math were evil jokes; why Constructivism is much ado about nothing; why every slogan used in the public schools—self-esteem, multiculturalism, and 25 others—

is really just an excuse to teach less. At some point, you'll be mad as hell, and you won't take it anymore.

———

Only Community Leaders Can Save Our Schools

In 2007 Bill Gates said the public schools are a threat to the nation's survival. It's important that community leaders become involved in what must be called a crisis. Your city needs you. It's easy to help. Here's how, in four steps:

I: START WITH A CLEAN INTELLECTUAL SLATE
Statistics trend ever downward: public schools have been sinking into mediocrity for 70+ years. It's clear that the people at the top are much too comfortable with mediocrity.

It's prudent to ignore the people who created all this decline. In short, start fresh. Find your own experts and your own answers. Become expert yourself.

II: TRUST ONLY THOSE PEOPLE WITH A RECORD of SUCCESS
Every city has three reservoirs of educational wisdom:
1. The people who manage private schools of various kinds.
2. Those in charge of good parochial schools.
3. Homeschooling parents.

(Note: homeschoolers have to spend all day at the kitchen table teaching. They don't waste time on methods that don't work, unlike public schools.)

III: SELECT THE BEST APPROACHES
Find out what goals and methods the most successful schools use. Support those methods!

You're a VIP. People will answer your questions. What values, what theories, what approaches, what curricula are mentioned again...and again?

In a few hours, you'll know what works and doesn't work. Here is a preview of what you'll probably learn.

BAD METHODS OFTEN FOUND IN BAD SCHOOLS:
Sight-Words, Dolch Words, High-Frequency Words, Et Al
Reform Math (12 varieties)
Constructivism
Cooperative Learning
Self-Esteem
Fuzziness
Social Studies
Guessing
Relevance
Multiculturalism
No Memorization
Pretend Critical Thinking
Disorderly Schools
Permissive About Breaking Rules, Cheating

Just a few of these ideas, used relentlessly, can cripple any school. Why? They rarely work as promised. And they have destructive side effects.

GOOD METHODS TYPICALLY EMBRACED BY GOOD SCHOOLS:
The 3 R's
Basics
Phonics
Arithmetic With Mastery
Cursive Handwriting
Facts
Knowledge
Academics
Aesop's Fables
Geography
Literature
General Science
History
Second Language
Homework
Proper Spelling

Accuracy
Promptness
Real Critical Thinking

IV: PUT ON THE PRESSURE

The blueprint for success is simple: discard the bad ideas, use only good methods. When in doubt, do what good schools do. Praise and promote those methods. Spotlight successful schools.

Conversely, explain and criticize what bad schools do. Publish their scores; name their principals.

Accept no excuses. When big organizations produce bad results, the top people should be replaced.

SUMMARY: public education, throughout the 20th century, was debased in order to achieve political goals. It's time to say goodbye to all that.

The best schools around the country, and throughout history, have done much the same things. Kids learn reading, writing, and arithmetic. From there they go on to geography, history, science, literature, and the arts.

————

Princeton, Harvard, and Yale Can Help Improve K-12 Education

I've had a pleasant fantasy where, circa 1955, the Chairmen of the Departments of English at Princeton, Harvard and Yale stand on the steps of Library of Congress and proclaim, "We support Rudolf Flesch!" This small gesture could have saved tens of millions of children from misery. But nobody from these places did a thing. Much to their shame.

In 1956 Flesch's enemies created the International Reading Association to discredit him, sabotage phonics, and keep Whole Word dominant. The damage continues.

Let's start with a safe generalization: our public schools are dumbing down multitudes of children. They can't read or write at an acceptable level, they don't know much history, science or anything else. All of this is empirically verified by tests of various kinds.

Even worse, all of this is anecdotally verified by millions of horror stories. A student at James Madison University, majoring in education, told me about a fellow student who didn't know who George Washington was. Note that JMU is in Virginia; and the ignorant student is a Virginian. I asked how is this even possible. The teller of the anecdote shrugged and said, "It happened, that's all I can tell you."

Who is going to protect those semi-educated kids? Who is going to say to our Education Establishment: enough already.

Most businesses and organizations don't have any special interest in intelligence or academic achievement. But the ones that do should take more interest in protecting public school students. For example, Princeton, Harvard, and Yale.

I'm been thinking about all the thousands of professors in all the colleges in the United States. What are they doing to help secondary education in America? Anything at all? We need these people to get out and fight, even if only a little.

For example, they could explain to their communities what's gone wrong in the public schools and why children receive such bad educations. They could explain why Flesch was right about reading in 1955 and still is. Professors could start making up for all the years when they were silent.

There are two factors for people in elite organizations to consider. First, all levels of education are connected. If public schools are doing a dreadful job, this mediocrity will wash over into colleges. The smart, self-serving thing for higher education is to be more protective of all education.

Second, the sophistries wrecking public schools are not that hard to understand. For example, you cannot teach children to read with Sight-Words. End of story. Flesch explained this impossibility in the simplest terms. But how many professors understand that statement?

There are a dozen main sophistries embedded in our public schools. Take a few minutes and you will understand why they are fake. For example, Reform Math is a concatenation of bad ways to teach math. "No mastery" is official doctrine. Contemplate the insanity of that.

Perhaps what we need is intellectual Big Brotherism. An awkward phrase but all it means is that elite organizations, especially ones with power, take a greater interest in the organizations lower down. Intellectual Big Brothers could issue statements, make demands, express solidarity, lean on society's leaders, and encourage children to aim higher.

Modern Language Association (MLA), National Association of Scholars (NAS), the American Historical Association (AHA), and similarly distinguished organizations should insist that public schools be improved.

The Chronicle of Higher Education should announce its own plan for helping K-12 education.

A lot of people remain confused about why Flesch was right in 1955. Maybe it's not too late for the Chairmen of the Departments of English at Princeton, Harvard and Yale to explain these matters. A press conference on the steps of the Library of Congress would be ideal.

———

Who Will Speak for the Children?

When children are not learning, where can parents look for answers? Who will tell the truth?

The experts, you say? The same people, you mean, who shaped and controlled the schools where these kids aren't learning? These experts do not inspire confidence. There are too many signs of failure and dysfunction. It's as if we glanced into the kitchen of a restaurant and saw insects scurrying on counters. No matter how fancy the decor, we may lose our appetites.

Clearly the experts have a conflict of interest. If they can't do a good job, are they going to tell us why? Aren't they more likely to make excuses and try to cover-up?

What we know for certain is that the USA spends more per capita than almost any other country But we still don't place well internationally. Mediocrity is our norm. We are paying for gold but getting tin.

There are many theories to explain our poor performance. The machinations of unions. The greed of publishers. The poor training of teachers. The indifference of parents. The schemes of ideologues. The lazy bad habits a monopoly or a cult might fall into. And simple dimwitted incompetence.

Even the possible explanations are scary. Probably it is better not to be distracted by the question of which factor is the most destructive. Probably all are working together.

So let's stay focused on the stats, i.e., the hard evidence showing that millions of children don't learn to read properly, don't learn to master arithmetic, and don't learn the most basic facts about this country or the world.

Once upon a time, an eighth-grade education meant that one had a substantial amount of learning. Now a high school diploma could mean that one has hardly any education at all. Students reach college with huge gaps in their knowledge.

Evidently, the Education Establishment has embraced theories and methods that are not the best choices. Some critics speak of schools deliberately dumbing down students. The tendency in general seems to be toward talking a good game, throwing around pretentious jargon, and doing the minimum that each community will tolerate.

The question that must haunt us is this: suppose our experts engaged in rigorous comparative testing and identified the best theories and methods. If we did things at a higher level, couldn't we easily lift every student 30, 40 or 50%? Add that up across the society, and we're talking about a Renaissance.

We have millions of children who are quickly classified as failing readers. If they were taught properly, they would be good readers. That's not a minor improvement; that's a vast improvement, from someone who is sub-literate to someone who can read a book for pleasure.

Who is destroying our schools from within? Are there ruthless social engineers trying to build a new world order. We have to ask them: where is it written that dumb societies do better?

In this complex, competitive world, the opposite would seem to be the case. We want our society to be as smart as possible. That can happen only if each student is as smart as possible.

There is a simple answer here. Americans need to demand a reversal. Away from dumb, toward smart. Every American must speak for the children.

It will be so easy to tell. In the second-grade kids are reading little books. In the third grade they are doing arithmetic. In the fourth grade, they know where their state is on a map of the country. In the fifth grade, they know who George Washington is.

Just the basic stuff. Nothing unreasonable. The problem now is that American children do not know basic stuff. They are in classrooms for years and years and years but by a perverse sort of alchemy, they learn virtually nothing. Aren't you sick of it?

10. WHAT TO DO NEXT

Suggestions for repairing the damage and taking back the schools.

Creating the Perfect School

As long as there have been schools, people have asked, "So, how would we create the perfect school??"

I think the answer is obvious. You would *not* do any of the things that our Education Establishment likes to do. Indeed, you would do the opposite.

I believe I know exactly what *they* would do. They would sweep through the Warehouse of Educational Fads, grabbing stuff off the shelves with giddy abandon. of course, their school would have Constructivism in all classes, with the teachers as Guides at Their Sides or, even worse, Facilitators. Lots of time would be wasted while students reinvent all of humanity's discoveries, and teachers ascertain each student's Prior Knowledge. Always, children would be encouraged to have deep discussions about the little they know, a fad called Critical Thinking. Meanwhile, the children would not learn to read, by using the method called Sight-Words. They would not learn how to do arithmetic, by studying the fad called Reform Math. They would be prohibited from really knowing anything, according to the doctrines of No-Memorization and No-Mastery. They would learn contempt for accuracy, according to the doctrine that praises Fuzziness. They would all get straight A's, according to the doctrine of Self-Esteem. They would be made to work in groups, never learning to work independently, according to the doctrine of Cooperative Learning. And to top it off, the faddists would brag that their school teaches 21st-Century Skills! Unfortunately, this last cliche refers collectively to all the other clichés already mentioned.

My own take is that all these fads are best understood as sound-good marketing slogans, more or less on the intellectual level of McDonald's *"i'm lovin' it."* Who could be against Self-Esteem? Cooperative Learning? Critical Thinking? Multiculturalism? Reform Math? Whole Language? 21st Century Skills? These artful slogans seem designed to make parents believe that something important is going on, and to convince students that they're not wasting their time at school.

Unfortunately, none of these fads is much concerned with content, substance, facts, or knowledge. Our Education Establishment has a long track record of being gaga about social engineering, but dismissive of intellectual engineering. Predictably, their schools are to education what scooters are to long-distance transportation. **As Professor Arthur Bestor noted more than 65 years ago, public schools will never get better, no matter who much money is spent, as long as the Education Establishment remains hostile to content.**

So, how do we create the perfect school, supposing we're serious about this quest? First of all, we start from a profound love of facts, and a reverence for knowledge. We proceed in a systematic way to teach foundational knowledge, and then to build on that knowledge, wider and higher. With the results that typical students in the seventh grade will know more than the high school graduates that the Education Establishment now turns out. Perhaps just as importantly, these young students will know what they don't know, unlike the so-called Critical Thinkers who are encouraged to believe they know everything they need to know.

Throughout history, all the good schools are virtually identical in having great seriousness of purpose. Without that, everything is a joke and a squandering of money.

The main improvement we can make on the past is to use the insight that you often accomplish more with carrots than with sticks. A smart school ensures that students have fun. They should look back and say, "Yeah, school was a blast." I think it's a matter of keeping things moving, of creating a wave of learning, of being deeply serious but having a light touch, of mixing sports and extracurricular activities in with the academic work, of mixing field trips in with the class work. Mainly, in the digital age we have so many more tools for memorable presentation of information.

I think really successful schools manage a sleight-of-hand, an intentional deception if you will, so that students don't realize that they're actually in a very intense academic environment. It surely helps a great deal if a school is like this from kindergarten onward. Young children, treated as little scholars, will grow into the part. They'll know that facts are fun, and knowledge is power.

Finally, the difference between the good school and the bad school is a matter of attitude and perspective. Good schools revere facts and knowledge, and want to inspire that feeling in children. Bad schools ricochet ineffectually from fad to theory to therapy, never committed to the reason that humans built schools in the first place: to transmit the best of the past to the future.

———

Ten Keys to Successful Teaching

Malkin Dare, a lifelong teacher and education reformer, is the founder of the Society for Quality Education in Ontario. She is a big voice for sane education in Canada and throughout the world.

Dare summarized her educational philosophy in a long article titled *Ten Keys to Success: Fundamental Principles of Teaching*. That article is condensed here to the main points (but always in Malkin Dare's words). Please, parents and teachers, read this material and put it into practice:

1. Almost all students can learn: Obviously, there are a few students who, because of a severe disability, are prevented from learning certain things. For the most part, however, students with conditions that affect their learning should be viewed as requiring teaching methods that enable them to overcome their difficulties, and the same high standards and bright future should be held out to them.

2. Almost anything can be learned: There are few, if any, people to whom all learning comes easily. Yet, given expert teaching and plenty of patience, almost everyone can achieve an adequate level of performance in almost any field—from ballet to physics to teaching prowess to drawing. Good teaching and high expectations can produce seeming miracles.

3. There are almost no circumstances under which students can't learn: Students who are experiencing physical or emotional discomfort can still learn; in fact, instruction can even help to take the students' minds off their problems for a while. It is an evasion of responsibility to assume that students can't learn if they are hungry or tired or upset about their parents' divorce. At Kobi Nazrul school in the slums of London, where the children are overwhelmingly poor and almost all are immigrants, the students score well above the national average and only three per cent of pupils are registered as having special needs.

4. Basic skills should be taught before higher-order skills: Basic skills, like sounding out unknown words or multiplying numbers, are the building blocks of learning. They must be in place before students can progress to higher-order skills, such as critical thinking and problem-solving. This is so obvious that it seems unnecessary even to mention.

5. Factual knowledge is important: The tendency these days is to de-emphasize the teaching of factual knowledge on the grounds that it is enough for students to be able to look up information (as opposed to knowing it). But skills are virtually useless in the absence of knowledge. Many educators worry that facts are soon outdated, but most basic knowledge, for example the elements of the periodic table or the date of the French Revolution, is unchanging.

6. Hard work must be encouraged: In North America, it is common to attribute success to innate ability, while in Asia success is generally thought to be the result of hard work. The difference has far-reaching consequences. North American students who think that they have low ability may give up before they start. In contrast, Asian students are often motivated to work very hard because they believe they can always do better if they work harder.

7. Lessons should be clear and precise: Teachers must know their subject thoroughly if they are to teach it effectively. A good command of the subject matter is necessary for a number of reasons, including the ability to explain the new concept clearly and concisely, to choose the most effective modes of presentation, to answer students' questions accurately, to devise the best methods of application and practice, and so on.

8. New concepts should be practiced until they have been completely mastered: The number of bits of information that the human mind can handle in the brief span of working (short-term) memory is very limited—five to nine items at most. The limitations of working memory mean that teachers must be careful not to overburden their students' capacity lest the presentation of too many demanding tasks simultaneously overwhelm them.

9. New concepts should be taught in sequence: The best way to teach complicated topics is to break the learning down into small pieces and teach them step by step in a logical sequence. After each new concept has been practiced and learned to the point of automaticity, the student is ready for the next one.

10. High student achievement is not dependent on lavish spending: Learning essentials are physical comfort, paper and pencil, freedom from distraction, reasonably homogeneous classrooms, manageable students, access to a library, and good teaching. Everything else is a luxury. Hundreds of comparative studies have found that student achievement is unrelated to inputs such as overall spending, class sizes, teachers' salaries, and computer purchases.

THE ESSENTIALS: Only one new item must be taught at a time. The new item must be explained with great precision and clarity, and the teacher must check to make sure that the learner understands the new concept. The student's mistakes must be corrected immediately. Short, separated-in-time practice sessions are most effective. The new learning must be revisited from time to time, ideally in application to and consolidation with other learning. The student must be praised and encouraged.

NOTE: material above is excerpted verbatim from Malkin Dare's article. Ellipses are not indicated. By permission of Malkin Dare.

French Class as the Paradigm for the Perfect Way to Teach Everything

There is one constant throughout the 20th century: professors of education came up with ever more exotic schemes for how education should be organized, even as the schemes confused students and destroyed achievement.

Each scheme had a catchy name (Open Classroom, Life Adjustment, Multiculturalism, Constructivism, etc.) and a phalanx of resistance-is-futile jargon. Somehow the proposal didn't translate into gains. One might cynically conclude that the jargon was a goal in itself (to get a grant, to build a career). You may even suspect that the larger purpose of all these schemes is to create an illusion of seriousness, and to fool parents into thinking that their children are being educated.

But what if we banished the nonsense, outlawed the jargon, and were genuinely serious, as opposed to faking it? What would that look like? Why, it would look exactly like what we see in every French class. And therein lies the starting point for this meditation.

Let's reflect on what is the most salient thing about a French class. Teachers and students start from a position of reverence for the material. French is a glorious thing. The students want to learn to speak French. Everybody's on board, with the same goal, the same love, the same seriousness. We want French and more French. We expect to make progress; and if we don't, we feel cheated.

The next most salient thing is that it's absurdly easy for an observer to judge the progress of the students. You say, "Ça va?" and they answer appropriately. You hand them a Parisian newspaper and they read it in a way that sounds like French. You say, "Here is an English sentence. Write it in French…Here is a list of French words, tell me what they mean." **See, the whole thing is totally transparent.**

I'll submit to you that ALL courses should be taught exactly the same way every good teacher naturally teaches French. That's the way things used to be done. I invite teachers to imagine how you would teach French if you were suddenly dropped into that position (assuming you speak French). Point is, you would be really serious about it. You would not settle for mumbo-jumbo and empty promises about what was supposedly happening. No, you would want your students to learn French! To read it, write it, and speak it, easily and fondly. What a utopian idea. But such actual mastery was the common practice in EVERY classroom until Progressive Education got in the way.

Respect for content and clear expectations, these are what our professors of education removed from arithmetic, history, and most other subjects. Content is regarded as a nuisance to be circumvented. Testing is dismissed or mocked. Nobody is actually expected to know even the most basic facts. There is merely the goal of spinning wheels, putting up a front, going through the motions. All of education becomes a strange sort of mime. Progress is not expected, and nobody knows whether they achieved any or not. Typically, classes are an incoherent blur.

Our elite educators managed to eliminate sequential progress and an honest evaluation thereof. All the while they injected cloudiness and incoherence into every subject. American History is reduced to dressing up as pilgrims and eating pumpkins. Being multicultural means that kids build models of pyramids and put on pharaoh costumes. Learning arithmetic is hopelessly befuddled, for one example, by spiraling from topic to topic. What kids need to know they don't master. A blizzard of trivial stuff smothers any chance of learning.

I suspect that, in the typical public school, the only courses left uninfected by dangerous fads are language courses. There, you would still see the focus on substance and goals that is the essence of education. You would still see the honesty—in school, teacher, textbook, and student—that is the precondition of learning. Finally, you would see the transparency that lets everyone quickly judge the progress of the class and of each student.

Good schools are so easily achieved! Everyone shut their eyes and imagine, in great detail, a good language class in a good school. All students are making progress each day. New vocabulary, improved accent, greater reading skills, everything building upward in a logical systematic way... Now, simply imagine that the same teacher is teaching European History, Biology, Math, or anything else. *Bingo.* That's the way you do it!

Good Teachers Must Unite

The following plea—written many decades years ago and addressed to all the teachers of America—is still solid gold today:

"You are a grade-school teacher. I know that you are doing a conscientious job, that you work overtime for very little pay, that you love children and are proud of your profession. Aren't you getting tired of being attacked and criticized all the time? Every second mother who comes in to talk to you tells you that she is dissatisfied, that her child doesn't seem to learn anything, that you should do your job in a different way, that you don't know

your business. Why should you be the scapegoat? The educators in their teachers' colleges and publishing offices think up all these fancy ideas, and you are on the firing line and have to take the consequences. Have another look at the system you are defending with so much effort. I know you are an intelligent young woman. You belong on the other side."

Rudolf Flesch wrote this in his 1955 bestseller "Why Johnny Can't Read." If anyone doubts it, Flesch is The Man in American education. Look at how perfectly he nails this vicious trap.

Nonsense cascades down from on high. Teachers are supposed to work with the unworkable, to live with the pathological consequences of letting muck into the classroom.

Flesch perfectly sums it up: You are intelligent. You belong on the other side. Please, come on over. Work to create real schools.

What would they look like? Simple. Every good school since the beginning of time has been more or less like all the others. Kids learn reading, writing, arithmetic, and geography, so they can move on quickly to history, science, literature, and the arts. It's not rocket science.

Sure, there are ideologues at Teachers College who would like you to think that it is rocket science. Their scheme, evidently, is to entangle and impede education, to make it difficult and tedious; and them to blame the bad results on everyone but themselves. They don't deserve your respect. Here are some simple steps for coming over to the Other Side:

1) **Recall that reading is half of everything.** Good schools have always taught children to read in the first grade. Does yours? (To accomplish this, you probably already sense that your school will need to eliminate all vestiges of Whole Word. Teach the alphabet in K, and phonics in 1st grade. Children should be picking books to read in 2nd grade.)

2) **The next most important goal is arithmetic.** Reform Math causes much more pain than gain. Get rid of it. REAL math is the answer. (If some "expert" tells you that kids don't need to know what 7 times 8 is, because they can use a calculator, you know you are talking to the problem.)

3) **Knowledge is king, or should be!** Public schools seem to do everything possible to discourage the actual acquisition of knowledge. Outwit this nonsense. Knowledge is the point.

4) Do not let them turn you into a facilitator. You are precisely the very thing they are most threatened by: a Sage on a Stage. That is your badge of honor and they want to take it away from you. They want to lock you into being an inferior teacher, diminished according to the dogmas of Self-Esteem, Cooperative Learning, Multiculturalism, Constructivism, Authentic Assessment, Portfolios, 21st Century skills and all the rest of the gimmicks.

5) Talk to teachers in private schools; find out what they are doing at the same grade level, and how they do it.

6) Talk to homeschooling parents. Find out why they are homeschooling, what their main complaints are, and what they are doing differently in their home schools.

7) Help the parents of your students to take back the school. The Education Establishment is not your natural ally. Parents and students are your allies. Work with them to improve the school.

Teachers are trapped in conditions that keep them from doing a good job. The Education Establishment is obsessed with social engineering, not intellectual engineering. **Good teachers know instinctively that the public schools could be much better. You can help make it happen.**

———

How to Improve Public Schools Without Spending More Money

It's generally agreed that the public schools are sub-par and could be much improved. But how?

Everyone seems to assume we need some big new concept, and who cares what it costs. We hear relentless shilling for Constructivism, 21st Century Skills, and now National Standards. Right on cue, Obama was out of the gate with Race to the Top, which is supposed to make kids College-Ready and Career-Ready. Excuse me. Could we first make them Book-Ready? And perhaps even High-School-Ready?

All of Obama's plans required billions of tax dollars. Why? Was there ever a correlation between money and quality? Well, perhaps there's an inverse correlation.

Here's what our Education Establishment is good at: concocting slick marketing slogans that don't produce results and then asking for raises all around. Enough.

We don't need any fancy slogans or ingenious new ways to waste more billions. I would argue that the proposals we hear mentioned again and again are beside the point, irrelevant, unnecessary, and probably harmful. All of these bogus ideas are expensive. They are also cumbersome; whereas the correct answer is inexpensive, and as simple as 1 + 2 = 3.

In fact, the correct answer is 1 + 2 = 3.

That's an example of basic or foundational knowledge, the kind of thing that every student needs to learn in the first years of school. Shazam!

As surely as 1 + 2 = 3, foundational knowledge is what we need to return to, immediately. Observe that no new laws are required. No new books. No new funding. No new training. No new schools or facilities. No new personnel. No new budget items of any kind.

We merely do again what all teachers automatically did for thousands of years. We teach the information that people need throughout their lives.

Sure, the anti-educators in charge of education have trashed this idea with so much cunning and for so long, you might mistakenly assume there is even a speck of sense in their objections. Not at all. Remember, these people are happiest when allowed to be social engineers. They don't have much feel for actual education. They wouldn't understand that foundational knowledge and education are more or less synonymous.

Teaching foundational knowledge is the right thing to do, the easy thing to do, the cheap thing to do. We'll return to the bright heart of education. Facts! Knowledge! We actually start to teach again. What an idea. This shift is so revolutionary, we might call it 22nd Century Skills.

No, no, we don't need to teach a lot. Don't be alarmed. We can teach almost nothing and still turn the country around. How about one fact each day?? Don't you think those little nervous systems can handle the stress of learning one fact each day? Personally, I believe their nervous systems would welcome the excitement. (I suspect a new fact each hour might work even better.)

What facts, you ask. Here's some more good news: it hardly matters. Any little bit of information you could reasonably call foundational knowledge, throw it out there to those fact-starved minds. You know, all that basic stuff that everyone really should learn, like how many quarts are in a gallon or how many days in a year. Ask yourself, is it something that the average adult ought to know? Then let's teach it.

There are three oceans—Atlantic, Pacific, and Indian. Any first-grader could handle that. The seven continents—everybody should know their names. The biggest river on each continent, how difficult is this? The highest mountain. Easy, right?

The twenty countries you're most likely to read about in the newspaper. The major capitals. Just keep it coming, at least one fact each day. All the facts mentioned so far don't add up to 200, which is the quota for first grade. What a beginning.

Second grade takes children up to 400 facts, third grade to 600 facts, which could reasonably include the multiplication table to 10 times 10. In fourth grade we're up to 800 facts, which might include the names of the 50 states. Heck, these student are ready to enter college by the standards of our public schools today.

All we hear now is complaints about "high stakes testing" and "teaching to the test" and how everybody is overwhelmed. I think this is dishonest propaganda. Here's what the real problem is. The kids in fifth and sixth grade don't know 25 facts, total. So how can anyone teach those kids American History, for example, when they don't know the names of oceans, mountains, states, rivers, etc.?

Here's a statement that must have occurred in thousands of history classes: "The Pilgrims left England and sailed westward across the Atlantic to Plymouth Rock." If you're educated, you think this is a trivial sentence. But it's not, not for the students in our public schools.

Here's what those kids are puzzling over: What are Pilgrims? What's *England*? What's *sailed*? What's *westward*? What's *Atlantic*? What's *Plymouth Rock*?

All that basic information might as well be most of us hearing about craters on Pluto. There's a perfect void. A teacher of American History hasn't got a chance. With no foundation to build on, teachers must spend all their time re-explaining the simplest things.

If children learned foundational knowledge in grades K-6, whatever came next would be relatively easy. American History is not that complicated but if the child doesn't know the name of the ocean next to the East Coast, what Columbus did, the names of the 13 original colonies, and what 1776 is, the whole year is an exercise in wasting time.

So much basic information has been stripped out of elementary education. There seems to be a deep hatred of knowledge. Is this whole thing a really bad dream? Imagine that some busybody like me shows up asking that one fact be taught each day. You'd *hope* that everybody in education exclaims: "Duh! of course!"

Nope. This proposal will actually strike our top educators as radical, something they need to ponder deeply. *Hmmm....*

I predict that our Education Establishment will sit around rubbing their chins and murmuring, "Maybe it's too difficult."

That's what we're up against. Ideally, we fire people aiming so low.

Until the public schools are intelligently run, the answer lies outside their walls. School-proof kids before they go to school. Prep kids during each summer. Hand out lists of websites on each subject. Subscribe to history and science magazines. Make a list of the museums, galleries, factories, and historical sites within driving distance—and visit one of them every few months. Basically, everybody needs to be, at least a little, in homeschooling mode. That movement started because the Education Establishment wouldn't do a good job. That's where we are today.

―――――

How We Fix the Public Schools ASAP In Four Steps

Lenin asked his famous question in 1901: "What is to be done"

Today in education, that question remains as hot and urgent as an oncoming typhoon.

The Education Establishment has spent 100 years making public schools dumber. That's a common impression which, after years of research, I could finally explain. John Dewey and his colleagues were in love with social engineering. In devotion to this passion, they were willing to throw almost everything else overboard. (You might think socialists could run good schools. But Dewey and his disciples fixated on a vision of empty brains, which the schools would fill in just the politically correct way.)

You can easily imagine that Dewey's approach will play havoc with education as traditionally understood. Dewey regarded that old-fashioned kind of education as, at best, a nuisance. And there, in that little sentence, you have 100 years of dumb and dumber.

So now, let's suppose that we had people in charge of education who understood that Dewey's non-education was a Vast Historical Detour, and now is a good time to put our schools back on track. What would they do?? Let's cut to the chase. Here's how we resurrect our public schools in just four easy steps:

1) SCHOOLS ARE SAFE AND SANE. Violence and disorder are not acceptable options. Students are asked to act with civility toward others. A strong principal (this is what I call the Principal Principle) should spell out what is expected of parents, teachers and students. Namely, constructive behavior. When discipline problems occur, there should be a clearly articulated spectrum of responses, from a friendly chat to calling the police. Everyone must know the school's expectations, and that if expectations are not met, the school's responses will increase in a predictable way. This is precisely what almost all students, teachers and parents are yearning for.

2) BASICS SKILLS AND FUNDAMENTAL KNOWLEDGE ARE TAUGHT. The Education Establishment scorns fundamental knowledge. Just as bad, the elite educators have promoted one counter-productive method after another. As a result of these unfortunate policies, the public is thoroughly confused about what can reasonably be taught and accomplished in school.

Let's imagine somebody was raised in the woods for 25 years and now wants to return to the ordinary world as a normal adult. **What information does that person need to know immediately?** There are hundreds of basic things such as the hours in the day, which way the North Pole is, what somebody is talking about when they say "the Nile." You start in pre-K and you teach the names of the oceans and continents. You work your way through the full range of basic knowledge. All of this goes right along with learning to read, learning to write, and learning arithmetic, a few steps each week. The goal is to give ordinary children a sense of confidence and comfort. Decide what an educated adult would ideally know; start teaching it the first day.

NOT doing this is the crazy, wasteful option. Every course after elementary school presupposes some foundational knowledge, some preliminary layers of information. For example, you can't teach

American History or World History if children don't already know the names of oceans, continents, major countries, rivers, etc.

The Education Establishment came up with methods whose true purpose seems not to be teaching, but stunting and retarding everything. One result is that we no longer know what ordinary kids are capable of. Let's teach them a little each day—slow, steady and systematic. I am sure that so-called ordinary kids will amaze us.

3) GOOD TEACHERS ARE NECESSARY. There are two ingredients. Teachers must major/minor in the subjects they will teach. Biology teachers must be expert at biology. Second, they must be comfortable speaking before any size crowd. Most of what happens now in schools of education should be eliminated as a waste of time. Instead, future teachers should spend months at Toastmasters, comedy training, or acting school, plus months of classroom training. Know your subject and feel comfortable explaining that subject in front of any kind of crowd, now you're a teacher.

4) TRANSPARENCY AND ACCOUNTABILITY ARE ESSENTIAL. The intent of the system is everything. Do the people in charge of the school sincerely intend it to be safe, secure, logical, and productive? Then it will happen. At the least, it can happen. Which is not the case if the people in charge have lesser goals and secret agenda. So the first step is to announce the real goals, rally support for them, and thereby make them a reality.

Of course you have quizzes and tests and papers. of course you have homework. of course you have a constant feedback from students so that they know how they're doing, so their parents know how they're doing, and so the teachers know how they are doing. All of these are aspects of transparency and accountability.

The rage against testing (which we have heard so much about for the past 50 years) was never about testing. The Education Establishment didn't want to teach facts and knowledge. To conceal the inevitable ignorance, the educators had to discredit tests.

IN SUMMARY: So much of modern public education is a distraction and a decoy. The parents and voters are given false choices to discuss and bad choices to vote on. Let's say you have an obese child. The Education Establishment would have us discussing whether to give the child ice cream, pie, or cake. No, all of those choices are bad. We first want to get the child in more athletic shape, with less eating and more exercise.

With regard to the schools, we first want to have them totally committed to a knowledge-based curriculum, openly explained and systematically pursued. This approach is quickly summed up with three words—Basics, Knowledge, Mastery.

Finally, a school's minimum necessary mission is to take each child as far as each child can go.

———

Sages on Stages Desperately Needed

It was the first premise of all schools throughout history: students would be educated by people who were themselves already educated. A biology teacher had to be an expert in biology; a history teacher must know history to teach history. Who would question the wisdom of these statements?

This country's Education Establishment now preaches a contrary view. Students must not be told that 2+4 = 6; this is not "authentic learning." Essentially, teachers are told to stop teaching. The theory, generally called Constructivism or Discovery, requires that students (typically working in groups) construct knowledge for themselves.

This approach gained traction in the 1980s and is now one of the central dogmas of progressive or modern education. Classrooms, we are told, should not be "teacher-centered" but "student-centered."

Traditionally, students were entitled to sages. But now the official slogan is: "We don't need sages on stages. We want guides at their sides."

In practice, teachers don't lead the class. Rather they become part of the class and wander among the students, nodding encouragement. As this philosophy has hardened, teachers have been rebranded as "facilitators." Increasingly, they are told to move to the back of the class and stay out of the way.

There are obvious problems. First, the person in the room who knows the most is forced to remain silent. Second, Constructivism, if it happens at all, will obviously be a slow process.

There are many simple facts (Paris is the capital of France) that can be taught directly in seconds. There are many complex phenomena (the origins of the French Revolution) that need to be explained at length. **Facilitators can neither teach directly nor explain at length.**

The general idea is that students will go to the Internet or other sources and figure out everything for themselves. You don't have to be a rocket scientist to conclude that the amount of knowledge transmitted per class will be drastically reduced.

Constructivism removes pressure from teachers to become expert in their subjects. Ed schools and administrators will ignore academic preparation even more than they did in the past, and instead focus on making sure facilitators have accepted their more passive roles. (*"Ms. Jones, you were teaching again. That's the third time this week. Knock it off."*)

In sum, Constructivism guarantees that teachers know less and children learn less.

It's as if all the dance instructors in the country had been recast as chaperones. How will anyone learn to dance? (Oh, that's right. They'll create the waltz by themselves.)

One result, which may still sound startling, is that students are constantly told to explain how they will solve a problem, as opposed to solving it. If students have a good strategy, they may get a good grade. The Education Establishment brags that it is no longer interested in the "what" but in the "how."

Everyone in education pretends these theories are new and exciting but most are warmed-over John Dewey. More than a century ago, he introduced the notions that children should be engaged in meaningful activities and should learn by experience. A little of this might be helpful. But now we've reached a situation where all teachers are expected to behave like Den Mothers in the Cub Scouts.

Surveys show that, across-the-board, Americans have scant general knowledge. Cynics say that constructivist theory is one big reason we have so much dumbing-down. As this policy is required, we can now properly use the phrase "deliberate dumbing down," as Charlotte Iserbyt put it.

It looks as if Constructivism will become more draconian in Common Core.

A teacher sent me this note: "I just read a post in a Charter School discussion group that basically said that Common Core State Standards require constructivist education...and that any teacher who didn't like it should be forced out of the profession or leave! There you have it.

And this woman works for a consulting firm which is paid by schools on how to evaluate teachers under CCSS!"

If you want to understand the folly of these methods just consider a real school: flying school, medical school, driving school, investing school, tattoo school, mountain climbing school, et al. Suppose the teacher refused to teach and instead told you to explain how you will find the answers. Predictably, you would demand your money back and run.

It's noteworthy that when grown-ups attend a high-end lecture, you can be sure there will be a sage on a stage, and a rapt audience guilty throughout of inauthentic learning!

Simply put, our Education Establishment doesn't want to teach geography, history, science, and all such old-fashioned knowledge. It wants to pretend to teach newfangled stuff such as critical thinking, creativity, digital literacy, and other buzzwords.

This whole slide toward nullity is disrupted only if at any point somebody insists on teaching something, learning something, or expecting somebody to know something. This is the reason we hear so much about "assessment and alignment." They want to teach as few morsels as possible, and then design tests that give an A to anyone knowing those morsels. The main thing seems to be to level everyone to average; and to keep the bodies moving through K-12 to college. There is a lot of money in education if the bodies are there.

What can the children do to protect themselves? Very little. It's up to the parents and community leaders to rescind these absurd fads. Otherwise, teach kids on the side, at home, and on weekends. By any means possible, go beyond what the school requires because the school often requires little.

Any genuine school reform demands a return to teaching. It requires a rejection of Constructivism as the all-purpose answer to everything.

What Should First-Graders Be Expected to Learn???

SUMMARY: Kids want to learn. There is no excuse for our schools to aim so low so often. Instead, start early and teach more. Our brains are wired for learning.

The history of American education for the past 100 years has been an exercise in chipping away at content. Or, more commonly, hacking away. Our top educators are good at coming up with excuses for teaching less and less.

Children are in school for 1,000 hours a year, or 12,000 hours from K to 12. With hardly any effort, children could learn a huge amount. Instead, schools provide busy-work but refuse to teach substance.

Just to turn this issue once again in the right direction, here's a suggested list of what can be taught in the first grade, EASILY AND TO ALL STUDENTS.

Remember that kids are in first grade for what must seem to them a lifetime. Why add insult to injury by keeping them as ignorant on the last day as on the first day?

OFF TO A GOOD START

The small amount of information listed below could easily be taught (always with lots of visuals) in the equivalent of a single day. Then you teach it again a month or so later, again a month later, and so on. That way, at the end of the year, the children know this information with almost no effort. Meanwhile, each child is learning to read and count, so now you have a child whose education is truly off to a good start.

GRADE 1: THE MINIMUM

The Sun—actually it's a small star—has eight planets going around it. The third planet from the Sun is called Earth. That's where we live.

Closer, we see Earth has three oceans, Atlantic, Pacific and Indian. (In fact, the North Pole area is nothing but water and could be called the Arctic Ocean; but it's almost always frozen so it's not usually referred to as an ocean.)

Earth has seven continents: North America, South America, Europe, Africa, Asia, Australia, and Antarctica.

First-graders should know the city and state they live in, and two or three nearby states, especially the ones mentioned in weather reports and local news. They should know the names of their own country and the neighboring countries, Canada and Mexico.

History is most easily taught by explaining the holidays as they occur: Columbus Day, Thanksgiving, Groundhog Day, Presidents' Day, etc.

General science: children learn that ice, water and steam are three states of same thing, and that water can become ice or heated to become steam. They know that snow falling out of the sky is the same as the ice in the refrigerator, and that the condensation on the window was, the minute before, invisible vapor.

Children should look at maps and diagrams whenever appropriate. One good example: a diagram of the classroom showing each desk, etc. (Maps, diagrams, drawings, and models are representations of something else. Practice with making and using such items is good preparation for almost every subject.)

That's it.

This list is simply a reasonable minimum. Probably, a great deal more could be taught to most children in the first grade. As Gilbert Highet (1906-1978), a great teacher, said: "No one knows, no one can even guess how much knowledge a child will want and, if it is presented in the right way, will digest."

LET'S BE PRO-KNOWLEDGE

In the second grade, the same material would be taught again but with obvious additions—more countries, the names of rivers and mountains, more historical events, etc. In this way, the child's knowledge base is widened and deepened in a coherent, systematic way.

Only one thing is needed to implement this simple plan, an Education Establishment that believes in education as the teaching of knowledge.

(This brief list can also serve as a handy litmus test. Educators who maintain that children don't need to learn this material reveal themselves to be anti-education. They are the problem we are trying to fix.)

What's the worst that can happen if you tell somebody about something new? They forget it. But probably not entirely. A trace remains. Then when you teach it again, they feel in control: *Yeah, I've heard about that.*

That's why the best strategy is to teach and teach again.

You may wonder why this article is necessary. That would probably indicate that your children go to a good school where they have to learn basic information. Lucky you. Lucky them.

Our national tragedy is that we have so many public schools which do NOT require children to learn facts. There is much chatter and make-believe; but in truth the schools simply do not believe in knowledge.

So I find myself insisting over and over that facts are fun and knowledge is power! I believe that any school built on those two ideas will automatically turn out to be a good school. Pass it on.

———

Good Education Manages to Look Easy

A century ago, Progressive education introduced a fundamental mistake into the public schools.

Basically, the mistake is that you do kids a favor by deleting content, diminishing substance, and simplifying everything as much as possible.

Here was the theory: if schools wanted all children to become more deeply involved in education, the best way to accomplish this feat was to make everything kid-friendly, simpler, more like a walk in the park than anything strenuous or difficult. The result was an ersatz kind of easy.

An interesting feature of these progressive ideas is that schools give up before the first day of school. There is total surrender, as if to say: These kids aren't very smart and probably won't learn much, so why make them feel bad?

Traditional classrooms aimed high, with the understanding that only some children would get A's. The rest of the class would master a portion of the material, and get B's, C's and D's. Everyone knew how well they had done.

So the progressive approach has two obvious drawbacks. Nobody is being pushed to go above a mediocre level. And nobody has any sure sense of where they stand. If every student has an A, which students have actually learned the subject? Nobody knows.

But the most profound flaw was noted at the beginning—that you should try to pull children into education by dumbing-down education. This is a glib superficial solution and finally a destructive one. If you dumb-down education, you will end up with millions of dumbed-down students. That is the outcome we are now living with.

The proper solution is to organize education so that it FEELS effortless to the students. The school aims high but is crafty and patient in reaching its goals. In short, good education appears to be easy education (not the painful chaotic mess we too often see now).

Let's look at the two approaches side-by-side. Suppose the subject is geography. The progressive classroom announces: learning the names of the states is a waste of time. The kids sigh with relief. They are kept busy learning nothing. Forty years later they are still paying for this dumbing-down.

The smart, effective school starts teaching the states in kindergarten and first grade. There is a lot of talk about one's hometown and state. And what about the states next to our state? And where have you traveled?

In second and third grade, teachers (often pointing to maps) introduce states still further away. Meanwhile, children are asked to draw the outline of their own state and nearby states.

So children are thoroughly saturated in American geography (let's say for an hour each week) in an ever widening spiral. By the fifth grade, most children would know the names of the states without even knowing they had learned them, in the same way they know the names of the football teams in the NFL.

And finally we reach the goal, in the seventh or eighth grade, where every student knows the states and can write the names on an outline map of the USA. If the school is crafty and patient, this is a very reasonable goal. Now children can be more effective students of history, environmental science, current events, and anything else.

The big point: these students would not have a sense of being burdened, of being asked to do something difficult. The educational process would happen almost without their knowing that it was happening. And this patient, incremental technique can be used in all of education. Kids can learn to count in the first grade by making change with pennies, nickels, dimes, and quarters. Children can learn history by learning about their own city and state. Events there give children a sense of time and place which can be transferred to other periods.

The fundamental strategy is to break subjects down into bite-sized morsels that every child can savor. You try to build a sense of momentum. You try to make kids feel like winners.

In every subject, for every class, there will be points of resistance where children start to doubt they understand what's going on. Teachers should back off, focus on something else, go around the point of resistance. The trick is to push but with flexibility and creativity.

Much more could be done in our schools but we seem to have people in charge who actually scorn education; so they come up with pretentious psychobabble in defense of methods that blatantly don't work.

Arguably, progressive theories are the kiss of death in the classroom. Most of the theories were devised to serve collectivism, not teaching, so we should not be surprised when learning suffers.

There is a science to teaching, to organizing and presenting material. This quest can be quantified in a loose way. Suppose you have 100 facts you want to teach to 100 kids in 100 days. What's the most efficient way to do this?? That`s a fascinating question! That's what our Education Establishment should be dealing with, as opposed to dreaming up a thousand excuses for doing nothing.

Conclusion: public schools seem to be designed to undermine children from every direction: reading, arithmetic, knowledge, attitudes. Americans should take back their schools.

SUMMING UP

We would like to think our Education Establishment is benevolent. Unfortunately, we have too much evidence to the contrary.

There have been patterns, readily apparent for a century, that our self-appointed experts have secret ideological goals. To fix our public schools, we have to understand these goals so we can work around them, or defeat them.

What is the simplest analysis of all? The public schools are mediocre because the people in charge *prefer* them that way. When you embrace that perspective, there is no mystery left. Everything makes complete sense. The elite educators are socialist busybodies, compulsive social engineers, people who think it's their right to conduct sociological and psychological experiments on your children.

If our self-appointed experts were serious about educating the country, they wouldn't impose a clunker like Whole Word on children. They wouldn't spring a disaster like New Math on every classroom. They wouldn't invent a gimmick like Constructivism in order to justify the end of teaching as we used to know it. They wouldn't launch a bogus array of identical courses, e.g., Reform Math, in order to confuse and demoralize opposition to their malevolent pedagogy. They wouldn't send a tsunami of goofy instruction, i.e., Common Core, flooding across the continent. They wouldn't concoct additional dozens of clever deceptions and sophistries that serve only to sabotage education.

If they insist, however, on committing these outrages, they should be held accountable.

Most Americans, glancing casually at the public-school situation, probably have a sense of unease. We feel the presence of too much that is counterproductive, perhaps dangerous, or even criminal. But how can anyone be sure? There seems to be a welter of contradictory opinions. So people tend to leave the situation alone. The Education Establishment gets a free pass.

How do our elite educators achieve this goal? The main technique is to create a swamp of semantic confusion. Productive discussion about education is virtually impossible. Here's why:

New theories and methods are continually announced and promoted. New possibilities are claimed and celebrated. New marketing slogans are constantly introduced. New jargon sprouts like mushrooms after rain. Additionally, many theories and methods have multiple names, much like Mafia criminals do. For example, Constructivism is also called Project-Based Learning, Discovery Method, Investigations, Inquiry, and others. (Meanwhile, the underlying trick is not mentioned: teachers must stop teaching.) In the case of reading, Sight-Words are also known as Look-say, word method, memory method, Whole Word, Dolch words, Fry words, Whole Language, Balanced Literacy, high-frequency words, and others. (Meanwhile, the underlying tragedy is not mentioned: phonics must be discarded.) The real action is hidden. What we see on the surface serves only to confuse us.

I would go so far as to say that no two Americans can have even a simple conversation about problems in the public schools. There is too much mumbo-jumbo, too many blurred lines. Each group of people has its own set of terms. Nothing is ever proved, disproved, or rejected. The Education Establishment seems to love ambiguity and incoherence.

———

This book's purpose is to inform people and thereby embolden them. As people learn more about the local school situation, they would be more likely to get involved. With greater public participation, there would be an irresistible tide in favor of better schools. People would demand traditional education, genuine education, effective education—whatever phrase you like.

The bad ideas so common in our school system are analogous to the viruses that people encounter on their computers. These things do not grow naturally, caused by the weather or solar flares. No, viruses appear in your computer for only one reason: some malevolent person puts them there, for money or to hurt you. That is an unpleasant thought. The good news is that a technician can easily remove those viruses one by one. Similarly, in K-12 education, the academic viruses have been put in play intentionally and they can be removed intentionally.

The simplest plan for reforming K-12 is to remove as many bad ideas as possible, and to bring back good ideas.

Just one change—children are taught to read with phonics in the first grade—would transform American education. We wouldn't have the vast waste on remedial interventions. We wouldn't have those years where nothing is accomplished.

Instead of teaching as little as possible, public schools could try to take education to a higher gear. This is easy to do.

This approach has to be better for individual students. It has to be better for the country.

There is so much waste and inefficiency in our public schools. I believe we could have much better schools at much less cost. Let's find out.

——*THE END*——

ABOUT THE AUTHOR

"Bruce Deitrick Price is a fierce advocate of education and in particular literacy instruction. A true believer in phonics instruction in early literacy, Bruce backs up his opinions with solid research and facts. His well-researched and thought-provoking articles are an asset for parents and educators alike. He is in a league of his own."
—Kim Latta, founder of Exceeding Reading

"There is nothing more important than your child's education, and no one has a better grasp on what is happening in the schools of the current day than columnist/author Bruce Price."
—Judi McLeod, Editor of Canada Free Press

"Bruce hits the nail on the head. Instead of improving curriculum and instruction, education has stepped up obfuscation and doubled down on excuses."
—Professor John Stone, President of Education Consumers Foundation

"I have always loved and admired these people. Samuel L Blumenfeld, Samuel T. Orton, Bruce Deitrick Price, Rudolf Flesch, John Taylor Gatto, Charlotte Iserbyt, Martin Kozloff, Charles Sykes, and Richard Mitchell."
—Holly S Muzzy, on her blog *Parents and Teachers against sight word memorization*

"When we have the good fortune to see a true warrior in children's education, we should mark that date on our calendar. We need to record the time we became amazed by the boldness, tenacity, and true creativity in that warrior's work. Bruce D. Price is one such warrior who continues to offer reason and truth to the expanding world of twisted education that our children and their parents must exist in every day."

—Nakonia (Niki) Hayes, author of *John Saxon's Story*, *a genius of common sense in math education*

"Education is our most valuable asset, an investment in our children and in the future of our world. Bruce Deitrick Price is a staunch supporter of this cause and produces some incredible work. Thank you, Bruce Deitrick Price."
—**Steven Farrell, Publisher of The Moral Liberal**

"I have fought for literacy for over 40 years, and am ever glad to find other people fighting with equal diligence, concerned with facts and understanding the simple needs. I hope everyone who reads this book, or anything else by Bruce Price, will join him. He is trying to restore normal life to thousands wrecked in government schools by mistrained teachers."
—**Mona McNee, author of The Great Reading Disaster and creator of Step-by-Step Phonics**

"You just have to admire this guy who for more than 25 years has been making reasoned and reasonable requests for better public education and, even though the education blob affects to ignore his attentions, Mr. Price refuses to shut up. It's because it's important, don't you know."
—**Malkin Dare, founder of Society for Quality Education**

"Bruce Price is one of the 10 people in the country who can explain what's going on in education."
—**Jonathon Moseley, attorney and host on Conservative Commando radio program**

"I greatly enjoy reading Bruce Price's informative articles, since my foremost interest has long been education. My wife of 46 years and I home educated all eight of our children while I was teaching college-level English and running an innovative program for homeschoolers, using many of the common-sense principles Bruce espouses. His insightful articles are educationally sound, timely, and relevant."
—**Stephen Stone, President of RenewAmerica.**

"Everything written by Bruce Deitrick Price about education is both lucid and compelling. He consistently sees through the jargon of the educrats and the longwindedness of John Dewey and other progressives, who are more interested in social engineering than in skills or independent thinking. He consistently makes a forceful case for phonics as being the best way to teach reading. This work is another example of his clarity and positive vision for American education."

—**Jeffrey Ludwig, author,** *The Catastrophic Decline of America's Public High Schools*

"Bruce Price has been successful in using modern media to reach a large audience with solid facts about the dangers of sight-words and the benefits of phonics-first. I once conducted an experiment when I Googled the term 'sight word' for 30 minutes and never encountered a single voice opposing them."

—**Don Potter, publisher of donpotter.net**

"Bruce D. Price is one of the nation's leading authorities on improving education. Bruce is a thorn in the side of the Education Establishment. His logic and ability to point out the blatant stupidity within the system have not exactly endeared him to the guardians of our failed education system, which is why I find Bruce to be a much needed and welcomed voice in fixing the country."

—**Tom White, publisher of VaRight**

OTHER BOOKS BY

Bruce Deitrick Price
(visit Lit4u.com)

Too Easy is a romantic/erotic thriller set in Manhattan. Kathy is sure that Robert belongs with her, never mind that he's married to Anne. Anne fights back. Hailed by Kinky Friedman as "the unwed mother of all page turners... so well-written it's frightening," Published by Simon & Schuster.

American Dreams was reviewed by *Publishers Weekly* as a traditional novel ("Price has written a funny, stylistically innovative novel that includes everything a popular novel should have: romance, sex, adultery, crime, religion, sickness, death and even Texas"). In fact, it's an experimental novel that uses techniques from the surrealists. There also similarities with John Cage and his random music; and William Burroughs and his cut-up technique. (See reviews on Amazon.)

The Man Who Falls In Love With His Wife is a romantic melodrama set in Manhattan. It asks the question, can a man love his wife too much?

Art and Beauty, a noir PI novel, is set in Manhattan in the 1980s when art galleries and modeling agencies were the most glamorous businesses in the world.

Big Dog is a retro PI novel set in Virginia Beach in 1970 as the Vietnam War was being lost. The author wondered, what would Raymond Chandler do with Virginia Beach?

Theoryland is a ten-page satire of academic excess. Price claims it's the best long poem in American literature, but admits there is not much competition in that category.

OTHER
ANAPHORA LITERARY
PRESS TITLES

PLJ: Interviews with Gene Ambaum and Corban Addison: VII:3, Fall 2015
Editor: Anna Faktorovich

Architecture of Being
By: Bruce Colbert

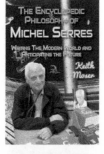

The Encyclopedic Philosophy of Michel Serres
By: Keith Moser

Forever Gentleman
By: Roland Colton

Janet Yellen
By: Marie Bussing-Burks

Diseases, Disorders, and Diagnoses of Historical Individuals
By: William J. Maloney

Armageddon at Maidan
By: Vasyl Baziv

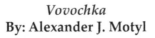

Vovochka
By: Alexander J. Motyl

9 781681 143613